D0752050

— THE —
ART OF STENCILLING

BY

LYN LE GRICE

Foreword by

H.R.H. PRINCESS MICHAEL OF KENT

Photographs by

DAVID CRIPPS

Clarkson N. Potter, Inc./Publishers

To Jeremy
for endless help and encouragement as ever

_____

For essential help in compiling this book I would thank
particularly: H.R.H. Princess Michael of Kent for being
so generous in agreeing to write the Foreword and for
being such an informative client; David Cripps, the
photographer, for applying his subtle skills in a diversity
of circumstances; Jessica Smith for her extremely
personal and dedicated approach in designing and pulling
this book into stylish shape; Catriona Luckhurst for
imposing her own calm order as editor; Liz Ardus for her
engaging secretarial help; Ben Pearce for his most
sensitive and patient assistance through the years in
turning stencil plans into reality; the clients for their
imagination, faith, understanding and generous
hospitality.
But most of all to Jeremy for his help and support of
every possible kind, and his unquenchable enthusiasm.

PUBLISHER'S NOTE
This book contains instructions for the use and application
of stencils. Reasonable care should be given to following the
instructions, especially regarding the use of paint, glue and
other potentially harmful materials.

Copyright © 1986 by Lyn Le Grice
Foreword copyright © 1986 by H.R.H. Princess Michael of Kent
Photographs copyright © 1986 by David Cripps

All rights reserved. No part of this book may be reproduced or transmitted
in any form or by any means, electronic or mechanical, including
photocopying, recording, or by any information storage and retrieval
system, without permission in writing from the publisher.

Published by Clarkson N. Potter, Inc., 201 East 50th Street, New York, New York 10022

Originally published in hardcover in Great Britain by Penguin Books Ltd., Harmondsworth, Middlesex, in 1986
and in the United States by Clarkson N. Potter, Inc., in 1987

CLARKSON N. POTTER, POTTER, and colophon are trademarks of Clarkson N. Potter, Inc.

Manufactured in Great Britain

Library of Congress Cataloging-in-Publication Data
Le Grice, Lyn
   The Art of Stencilling.
   1. Le Grice, Lyn.   2. Stencil Work – England –
History - 20th Century. I. Title
NK8667.L4A4   1987   745.7'3'0924   86-12230

ISBN 0-517-58016-0

10 9 8 7 6 5 4 3 2 1

First American Paperback Edition

CONTENTS

H.R.H. PRINCESS MICHAEL OF KENT

When Lyn Le Grice first came into my life, I thought stencilling was something the children did. And indeed it is. Simplicity has never been a drawback to originality or pleasing design, as the earliest stencils on cave walls show. I myself am attracted by the two-dimensional quality of *painted* repeated patterns, eliminating that 'dead' feeling paper borders so often have. Some years ago we bought a large old Cotswold house whose exterior grand classical proportions masked the local craftsmen's wobbly walls inside. The gloomy north-facing staircase, four stories high, cried out for a pattern and sunshine colours (no wonder there were rumours of ghosts), but no wallpaper could ever be matched against the eccentric undulations of its surface. I saw Lyn's work in a magazine and consulted her. As an interior designer, I had some ideas of my own, and what I suggested must have truly dismayed her in its complicated intricacy, but the result is a triumph – yellow watered-silk 'damask' walls which no one believes have been stencilled.

The methods and techniques described by Lyn in this informative and instructive book illustrate well that everyone has a place for stencilling somewhere in his or her home, as well as demonstrating how easy it is to try oneself. It is also particularly pleasing, in these days of mass production and mechanical techniques, to find old crafts being revived with such taste and skill as Lyn Le Grice has done with stencilling.

STENCILLING AS A TRADITIONAL ART

An enamel porridge bowl: is that my first memory of the versatile stencil? Or a child's stencilling pack, exuding the smell of the linseed-oiled paper as the lid was lifted off the flat cardboard box? I remember the feel of the machine-cut design and the unsuitable harshness of the bristle brush, which never produced the clear surface of colour and the crisp edge that I wanted. The memory remains of the pleasure of drinking from generous French coffee bowls with round-petalled flowers or eating off Portuguese platters sparsely scattered with bottle-green leaves and mulberry-coloured grapes.

Stencilled imagery, always recognizable by its formal structural divisions, is seen in varied and unexpected contexts. At its most utilitarian it marks out brands and symbols on the jade tarpaulins of European juggernauts. It is found brightening the kitchen shelves of young homemakers on enamelled domestic ware from Poland and China. It can be seen on the rough wooden casing of presentation tea-chests, decorated with palms and coolies, or on black lacquered souvenir trays with gilded birds among branches and camellia blooms, cheap treasures brought home by early nineteenth-century sailors.

Stencilled imprints may also be seen in the form of pale and delicate wistaria and butterflies on a cotton kimono, or a richer fragment of Persian silk hanging on a museum wall. Pale and powdery stencilled murals tell of the once colourful embellishments of our medieval churches and halls, whose imagery taught the illiterate faithful the lessons of the Bible, while manuscripts and psalters for the literate were illuminated with decorative stencilling.

This fleeting succession of images merely indicates the resilience and diversity of a method that extends far back into history, to the ancient civilizations of China, Japan and Persia, and back still further to the cave art of prehistoric man. In the caves of Lascaux in France a human hand was used as a living stencil, outstretched fingers daubed around with earth colour, serving perhaps as some primitive form of signature.

Opposite: *A nineteenth-century Japanese stencilled kimono.*

Below left: *A prehistoric 'stencilled' hand from the Lascaux caves.* Below right:

A stencilled tea-chest with the original metal stencil in place, centre.

9

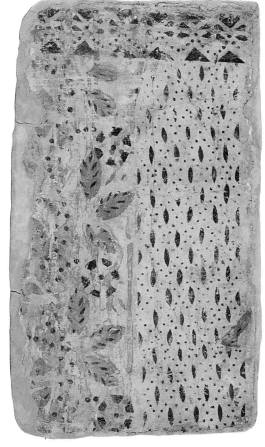

Opposite: *A stencilled panel in the Castle Museum, Colchester.* Above: *The Commandery Chapel, Worcester; top: a detail showing more clearly the red stencilled flowers of the background.* Right: *A stencilled panel at Saffron Walden, in delicate hues.*

Early English stencilling was such an unexceptional and under-prized practice that few records of it remain. Visual evidence is also rare: the rich patterns and colours that decorated the medieval churches and halls of the thirteenth and fourteenth centuries have been almost completely erased by the passage of time. However, by the fifteenth century there is material proof that the stencil was used as a device by which to repeat the pure pattern-work that was part of these interiors. In imitation of the richness of gilded brocades, patterns were transferred by applying, through the stencil, a gluey varnish to plaster and wood, which were then powdered over with gold and other heraldic colours in pigment form. An exquisite example of this process is still to be found on thirteen panels of a rood-screen in the parish church of Ranworth, Norfolk. Here the *primavera*-like pattern of the golden flowers is formally stencilled across the dark-green ground, which provides a setting of great beauty for the finely executed saintly figures. Further fluent stencilling is to be found in the foliage on the panelled surrounds, imparting a strangely three-dimensional quality.

In the small whitewashed Chapel of the Templars' Commandery of St Wulstan in Worcester, a medieval wall painting was uncovered in the 1930s, depicting St Michael weighing souls (see p. 11). Stencilled dominantly across the whole of the background of this extraordinary scene is a large, repeated, formalized flower, interspersed with a smaller conventionalized flowerhead. The Hospice of St Cross at Winchester is recorded as having walls with 'stencilled pattern on the surface itself', thought to be work carried out for Cardinal Beaufort in 1500. Both these examples seem to typify the use of the stencil during this period, forming as they do a background of regular patterns behind symbolic religious figures.

In the early 1500s, we see an increase in the use of the stencil, for, in addition to its place in religious houses, there is evidence that it moved into the scholastic world. Examples, similar in their nature to those of the stencilled patterns at St Cross, are recorded as being found at the colleges of Christ Church in Oxford and Trinity in Cambridge. At Christ Church the design was carried out on wallpaper, stamped 1509, and at Trinity the stencilling was applied directly to the plastered surface.

In Tudor and Jacobean times, the stencil was employed in order to create simple schemes of ornament and to break up the ground of the walls into panels. Designs were built up from simple forms of squares and lozenges and, where the design was more complex, the stencil was reversed from panel to panel. In the Castle Museum at Colchester, something of a centre for the preservation of early stencil work, there is a fine example (see p. 10).

In nearby Saffron Walden, there is another more complex example of the East Anglian penchant for the stencil, in which a more intricate pattern is achieved by superimposing a secondary colour, green upon paler green, to achieve the effect of veined foliage (see p. 11).

The popularity of stencilling as a secular art was to be short-lived, for it posed such a threat to the powerful Painters' and Stationers' Company of London that it caused the Company to declare the art 'a false and deceiptful work and destructive to the art of painting, being a great hinderance of ingenuity and a cherisher of idleness and laziness in all beginners of the said art'. This was obviously an outrageous piece of propaganda, for, on the contrary, the stencil is clearly a tool of great ingenuity and, indeed, often demands considerable stamina in its use. Was it an expression of some fear that, once the cut design found itself in unskilled hands, these hands would prove unexpectedly adept and the practised hands of the master craftsman would be left unemployed and idle? The company must have wielded considerable influence – or was it merely coincidental that stencil decoration faded from the scene for almost a century, apart from a small pocket of East Anglia where its use seems to have endured with particular tenacity?

Travelling west to Somerset one comes to another area where early stencilling is recorded. That records are available is due mainly to James Ayres, a scholar of vernacular interiors who has made meticulous records of half a dozen interiors in and around Bath. It is interesting to note that, in the main, these are not principal rooms but small, intimate back rooms with fragile, dappled interiors, rooms that could have been described with care by Jane Austen as apt settings for her pensive heroines. Mr Ayres has in his collection a remarkably fine stretch of matchboarding dated 1840 – stencilled with fragments of blues and overstencilled with coral on a pink ground – rescued from a house in Sharpstone, Freshford, near Bath (see p. 11). This simple domestic use of the stencil is described in Loudon's *Encyclopaedia of Cottage, Farm and Villa Architecture* of 1836 as 'not unsuitable for cottages of the humblest description, on account of its cheapness; and because, in remote places, or in new countries, it might be done by the cottager himself or by the local plasterer or housepainter'.

Canvas paintings being the prerogative of the rich, householders of more modest means turned to decorated papers instead. These papers were first produced in woodblocked squares of pattern and were used for lining niches, cupboards and chests; a natural development was for individually stencilled squares to be joined together to form twelve-foot lengths and applied, in adjoining strips, to entire walls. The first wallpapers were stencilled in imitation of cloth in order to recreate the illusion of the luxury of rooms hung with tapestries and floral brocades. The old practice of using leather or oilcloth stencils for applying the glue to a surface was revived, but instead of applying particles of gold to the tracery of sticky patterning, powdered shearings of wool were scattered over it, resulting in the unique plush, tactile finish of flocked wallpaper.

In addition, stencils were also brought in as a means by which to print pure blocks of colour on papers, which were then further overworked with woodblocks with representational outlines of birds, fruit and flowers – imagery that evoked woven Spitalfields silks. The craftsmen soon became so skilled

in the manipulation of pure stencilled blocks of colour that eventually designs were created that were elaborate enough in themselves to stand alone without the overprinting. A supreme example of this singular skill was found in Colchester, where a room of Holly Trees House was papered with a magnificently robust design. A tree of life with solidly curling leaves, reminiscent of crewel-work, grows from a base of tussocks in beautiful blues and ochre, and this is accompanied by a pole furled with smaller leaves, which forms the border that brims the top.

Stencilled wallpaper was introduced because its cost compared so favourably with that of cloth (even in the 1740s, cut velvet was twenty-five shillings a yard and damask twelve shillings a yard, by comparison with flocked wallpaper, which was four shillings a yard), but ironically its very popularity led to its demise, as the growing demand for patterned paper prompted the invention of cheaper and more highly mechanized processes. For while the stencilled paper at Holly Trees stands as a splendid emblem of the stenciller's art, with all its colour variations, it must have been excessively expensive to produce. There are excellent examples of seventeenth-, eighteenth- and nineteenth-century stencilled wallpaper in the Victoria and Albert Museum, including fragments from The Grove in Highgate and Clandon Park in Surrey (see p. 14).

However, the gentle art of stencilling did not die out completely in Victorian England, geared as it was to mechanization and mass production. Influential voices, like those of Pugin, Ruskin and Morris, were raised against the squandering of the craftsman's traditional skills, and stencilling reappeared in the interiors of adherents of the Arts and Crafts Movement. The architect William Burges saw the decorative potential of the stencil and used it to great effect both in his interiors and on furniture, examples of which can be seen in the Victoria and Albert Museum. On one piece one finds a stencilled row of golden hedgehogs, snout to snout, and on another, facing each other on the cupboard door, a pair of

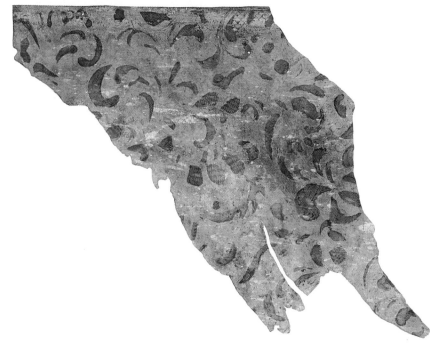

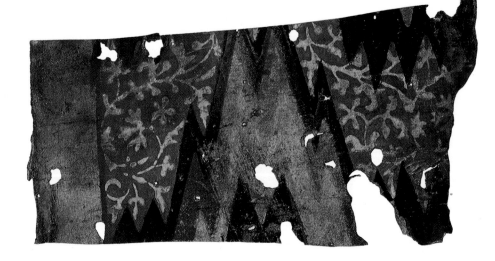

14

Opposite, far left: *The edge of a piece of stencilled matchboarding, c. 1840.* Opposite: *Fragments of eighteenth- and nineteenth-century stencilled wallpaper in the Victoria and Albert Museum.* Right: *A strongly coloured stencilled chest of drawers by William Burges.*

ferocious dogs, labelled 'Beware' and 'I bite', a veiled warning to prying fingers (see below).

Having chosen to include a particular Burges stencil design in this book, I was delighted to discover at a London antiques fair the actual piece of furniture on which it was used (see p. 15). A plain and unremarkable chest of drawers is transformed into something far more distinguished by stencilled decorations in yellow on a brick-red ground, a colour combination that evokes the richness of medieval gilding. The inset portrait panels by Charles Rossiter add to the charm of the chest, showing a smock-clad rustic on one side and a dandified city-dweller on the other. It is interesting to note that part of the rough design has been pounced, that is, finely perforated along its outlines so that, when placed on another surface, it can be dusted with chalk or charcoal to leave behind a dotted impression of the design.

The movement which adopted stencilling most wholeheartedly towards the end of the last century was that of Art Nouveau. The unique and controversial talents of Charles Rennie Mackintosh and his partners, in the group known as the Glasgow Four, produced strange and unconventional stencilled images like those commissioned for Miss Cranston's tea-rooms in Glasgow. The elongated backs of the chairs made for the Rose Tree tea-rooms are stencilled with a Celtic conception of that flower, while stencilled banners, showing roses entwined round the highly stylized figure of a woman, decorate the walls. The group's exhibits at the Arts and Craft Exhibition of 1896 were received at first with shock and disdain; although he eventually gained general recognition, Mackintosh was always more appreciated in Europe than in his own country.

Left: *Stencilled furniture decorations by William Burges:* above, *Burges's drawing for the stencilled chest of drawers shown on page 15;* centre, *one of his stencilled hedgehogs;* below, *the two dogs with their warning labels.*
Opposite, left: *A chair with stencilled back by Charles Rennie Mackintosh.* Opposite, right: *Miss Cranston's tea-rooms, Glasgow.*

No survey of the stenciller's art can overlook the remarkable work of the early settlers on the east coast of America. Far away from the fabrics, carpets and wallpapers of their homelands, they appeased their thirst for pattern and decoration by creating their own designs. Walls, floors, windows and domestic paraphernalia were embellished with such country imagery as baskets of strawberries, plums, apples and pears (the symbols of high summer brought in to help soften the rigours of the harsh winters). Beehives and birds, cornucopias of fruits were strewn across coverlets, chairs and chests, endowing them with a quality beyond their humble construction.

Because of their limited access to more sophisticated pigments, the stencillers formed their own particular set of primary colours. The natural dyes, which were mixed into a paste with whey, were quite unlike the exotic ultramarine, vermilion and cadmium favoured by the mannered European society of the time, but they had a mellow richness of their own. Stencillers had no inhibitions regarding what was currently tasteful or suitable, isolated as they were from such opinions, and their enthusiasms resulted in decoration of a naive charm. What they had on their side was time, and, given time, a great deal can be achieved with very modest materials.

18

Opposite: *American
'theorem' pictures.* Right:
*The stencilled backs of three
chairs, two of them (top and
bottom) from Hitchcockville.*

The popularity of stencil decoration grew as communities prospered, and there emerged a band of travelling craftsmen who moved from settlement to settlement armed with the modest tools of their trade. Together with the lady of the house, these craftsmen would devise schemes to transform the bare walls with panels and borders, reserving the area above the mantelpiece for the most important stencils. Any piece of simple furniture could be enlivened by the stenciller, from chairs and chests to clocks and picture frames. The characteristic images of ripe fruit and flowers themselves became subjects to be framed: the elaborate compositions that were built up of overlaid stencils, one for each colour, on a background of peach-bloom velvet were called 'theorems'.

But inevitably, as happened in Britain, the craftsmen could not cope with the increasing demand for decoration, and machine-produced wallpaper, carpets and fabrics soon obscured the delicate stencilled images of the earlier generation. However, mass production did make a positive mark in the world of stencilling. A whole town in Connecticut grew up around a factory making stencilled chairs, taking its name, Hitchcockville, from the owner Lambert Hitchcock. The elaborate chairs were stencilled by a highly skilled workforce, which included women, who decorated the shapely backs and struts of the chairs with baskets of fruit, flowers and leaves, burnished with copper and gold metallic paint. These sturdy but decorative chairs were shipped all over America in kit form, to be assembled as symbols of elegance in unsophisticated surroundings. Their design was a curious mixture of European styles, borrowing a little from Sheraton, a little from Hepplewhite, and succeeded in looking like something from the French Empire. The excitement caused today by the discovery of a chair stamped with the name of Hitchcock makes it hard to imagine that these chairs were mass-produced to furnish the houses and meeting places of the poor and emerging communities of the New World.

This period of American history, with its attendant arts and crafts, is recreated in a number of museums along the eastern seaboard of the United States. There is, for example, a particularly ravishing stencilled house that forms part of the Shelburne Museum in Vermont, and at Old Sturbridge Village

Below left: *A decorated chair against the stencilled panelling, shown in greater detail,* opposite, below, *where the broken texture of the wall adds richness.* Below right: *A detail of the lavishly coloured bedspread.*

Opposite, above: *A room decorated with stencils in the American Museum in Bath.*

in Massachusetts there are several stencilled rooms. But perhaps the most imaginative presentation of a whole way of life is at Claverton Manor, the American Museum near Bath, where many examples of the flowering of American folk-art are to be admired in carefully reconstructed room settings. It was my visit to this treasure house that first aroused my interest in stencilling and opened my eyes to its astonishing decorative possibilities.

While the early years of this century saw the flourishing of numerous workshops and studios in the Arts and Crafts tradition, whose craftsmen numbered stencilling among their skills, the revival was short-lived. The Modernist movement of the inter-war years brought with it the fashion for pristine white walls and interiors in which two-dimensional patterns played no part. With a few exceptions, such as the neatly stencilled 1930s tiles to be seen at the Ironbridge Tile Museum or the Minton 'Solarno Ware' crockery of the same period, for almost half a century the stencil's use has been largely utilitarian: farm sacks, tea chests and road markings are common applications of the process.

It is in the refreshing nature of fashion that we now see the hand-stencilled wall providing a surface of rare and coveted luxury.

STENCILLING FOR MYSELF

A Gloucestershire Stone Barn

My first experiments with designing patterns for walls were very tentative. It was not with stencils that I worked first but with simple flowerheads, cut into the tops of different-sized corks, which I dipped into indigo ink and applied evenly around windows and doors on to the ochre-painted walls and the painted interiors of cupboards. This timid first step broke down my resistance to using the wall as a surface for design.

We were in the process of converting a lovely Gloucestershire stone barn into our home and, by the time we moved in, I had gained the freedom to build on my tentative beginnings in decoration. The way in which we were restructuring the building for living, designing it on the kitchen table and altering it in stages, allowed for a very personal approach. This quality was further enhanced by my discovery of the use of spray paint in conjunction with stencils. It was the direct and tactile qualities of stencilling that made it so right. With this method it was possible to create decoration which had an unpretentious quality achieved through simple and economic means.

Opposite: *Our stone barn, set in a wooded Cotswold valley.*

Below: *A frieze of wheat on the kitchen worktop.*

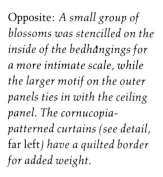

Opposite: *A small group of blossoms was stencilled on the inside of the bedhangings for a more intimate scale, while the larger motif on the outer panels ties in with the ceiling panel. The cornucopia-patterned curtains (see detail, far left) have a quilted border for added weight.*

The carving at the base of the mirror, above, *inspired the motif,* right. *It was used to frame the headboard,* bottom left, *and reversed on drawer fronts,* bottom right.

Anna's Bedroom

It was in Anna's bedroom that I chose to start stencilling. The timbers were exposed; the ceiling reached up to the ridge of the roof and there was a large area of newly applied plaster with marvellous texture and natural pink colouring. I stencilled this sparsely with a robust flower motif drawn from the wooden carving of the dressing-table mirror. I found the plain plaster of the walls beautifully receptive to stencilling, which gave a surface quality totally different from wallpaper. While the stencil paint itself was tough, the surface of the plaster was more porous and therefore needed protection, for which I used a water-based clear glaze with a matt finish. I later heard that one can protect such walls with a coat of beeswax and wished I had used it here.

I found that I could print very easily from the same stencil on to the calico curtains that were to be hung behind and at each side of the bed. After washing to shrink and carefully ironing the lengths of un-bleached calico, I stretched one across the kitchen table. I then measured off the areas I wanted to stencil, checking the placing of the design. I found that one of the advantages of stencilling cloth was that a design can be made specifically to fit a given area and shape; usually with cloth you have to take the repeats as they come. In this case I was able to print off a stencil of an elaborate bowl filled with pears in the centre of the back curtain and to repeat it at the base of each of the side hangings. A horn of fruit, pineapples, grapes and pears was applied to the canopy of the bed and also used on the window curtains. A tall pine chest of drawers was decorated in a simple manner with the original flower stencil, repeated between the handles of each drawer. The effect created an illusion of a certain unassuming country grandeur.

Border for a Passage

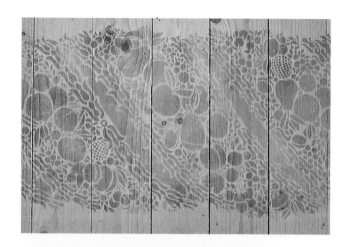

Leading to Anna's room was a long corridor with a newly laid wooden floor. Rather than carpeting it, we decided to decorate it with a stencil. I designed a rolling border of fruits and berries edging the walkway and riding up over the three stairs at the end. With its strange fruit, pomegranates or lychees, placed close against the small intricate shapes of the leaves on either side of a ribbon, it was a densely packed design that required intricate cutting, a feat demanding tenacity, I found, rather than any particular skill. The stencil was set four inches from the walls and had the immediate appearance of being in one colour, Venetian red, although when the sun struck across it, one could see that the fruits were shaded with a mellow bronze. We dappled the walls of the passage a strong pink to complement the colours on the floor, leaving an unpainted line to border these walls.

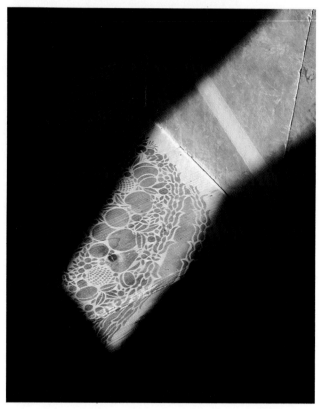

The earth-red used for this broad border, above and opposite, links up with the terracottas in Anna's room. The borders surrounding the slit windows, left, were achieved with the aid of masking tape, which was removed after the walls had been daubed with paint.

The Top Bathroom

The bathroom in the long pink passage was built up into the roof in order to clear the highest of the large barn doors and leave the original through passageway clear beneath it; consequently its windows were at floor level. The light from these windows was muted and mysterious, but the view was limited.

Because this room was partially closed to the green world outside, I felt that the stencilling could be quite exuberant. Calling on a more artificial range of colours, I used stencils of escapist imagery, exotic flowers, fruit, birds and fans, coloured in vivid reds, yellows, pinks, purples and acid greens. The everyday business of taking a bath was here transformed into a sensuous experience.

Huge medieval beams determined the unusual position of the dado border, above and opposite. Incidental stencils, like the pheasant, left, were placed above the beam to counterbalance the border's powerful scale.

Autumn mists and late springs gradually made the initial quiet and subtle colouring of our bedroom seem pallid. I would lie there wondering why we seemed so timid with colour in England, why we could not employ some brilliant hues from the brighter shores of the Mediterranean as an antidote to our gentle climate. So I chose veridian green, deep, sharp pinks and clear, clean blues to stencil lilies and butterflies, ribbons and fronds of leaves on to walls we had mottled to look like creamy old plaster. The doors and deep-set windows were painted in veridian and streaked with softer greens. The effect was elevating – colours beautifully muted on dull days or vividly glowing in sunlight.

The low frieze in this room also forms a frame around the top of the bed, enclosing sprays of lilies and butterflies, below *and* left.

Opposite: *Because of the weight of the stone sill, I stencilled only a delicate border of ribbon beneath the window.*

To fill the irregularly shaped panels in this room, single branches of the border foliage were used, below, left *and*

opposite. *The narrow space around shelves was decorated with just a strand of ribbon,* bottom.

The small bathroom leading off this room shared the same border stencil of ribbons and leaves, but the colour of the ribbon discreetly changed from pinks to blues. The walls here were blue too, not flatly painted but watery and full of movement, reflecting the changing light from the big window over the bath. The bird-cages stencilled on the wall had open doors, the birds flying freely, and used images I had seen in one of the magnificently painted rooms of the Palais des Papes at Avignon. There the cages were painted into the deep window recesses of one room; those rooms are gorgeously inventive and were for me an exciting and inspiring discovery.

Left: *The initials of the girls who shared this room are worked into the strawberry pattern.*

Opposite: *Because of all the clutter in a child's room, I concentrated the stencilling on one wall, top left, with just some palm trees set back by the window. Each animal stencil was reversed, centre, but I should have made two separate stencils for a lion and a lioness, right.*

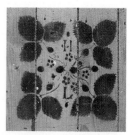

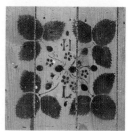

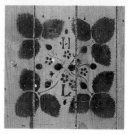

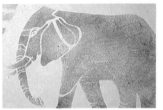

Harriet's and Louise's Room

I designed the decoration for a floor in one of the bedrooms after an exuberant day's strawberry picking with the children. It occurred to me that the berries and leaves of the plants would make an appealing motif for their room. The new wood of the floorboards presented such an ideal surface it would have been foolish to hide it. I brought back with me from the fields some leaves from the strawberry plants, and sat down and drew them to scale, using them almost like stencils and gradually working them into a design for the floor. I set the leaves within the edge of a twelve-inch square, added a handful of wild strawberries with their flowers and included the initials of Harriet and Louise who shared the room.

The tile-shaped stencil was easily repeated to form a border around the room, and a further three units were set side by side in the window seat. The hard, dark-green of the leaves stood out well against the yellow of the floorboards, and the crimson of the strawberries seemed to stain the wood. In retrospect I regret that the strawberry flowers were not painted in in white, as this could easily have been done before the floor was varnished.

Jude's Room

Photographs and a very well-drawn children's book provided me with the detailing for the foreign animals in Jude's Noah's Ark, and I drew the ark and Noah from my own head. The dove was drawn from an enlarged detail in an embroidery, and I cut the clouds, rainbow and raindrops straight into the stencil card surrounding the ark (also making a single raindrop to apply where I felt it was needed for balance). The colour scheme for the whole wall developed from the soft tones of the rainbow. A pictorial motif, such as this, lends itself admirably to stencilling, as the animals can be repeated straight-forwardly, or reversed and repeated.

The Cloakroom

Wells Head is set in a wooded valley. It is not surprising that the surrounding trees influenced my stencils with their leaf-forms and fruits.

I stencilled a small cloakroom with a theme taken from the English oak, its leaves and acorns making a border and the generous shape of the tree itself a strong central motif. It seemed appropriate to add a pair of placid Cotswold sheep, grazing beneath the leaves. To avoid a cloying naturalism, I sprayed the leaves a faded Prussian blue (not unlike denim) and the acorns an astringent golden yellow; the sheep remained a realistic ivory on grass-green bases.

Where the frieze ran along irregularly shaped beams, the stencilled image succeeded in looking most apt. No strangely curling corners of unevenly cut patterned wallpaper here, just the stencil on the plaster abutting the wood.

The wooden end of the light cord, below, *suggested both the motif and the position of the individual acorn clusters. The surface of the door,* left *and* below left, *and of the corner cupboard,* opposite, *was roughly broken up by three colours to imitate the appearance of old wood.*

Downstairs the kitchen required little by way of decoration to add to its atmosphere; indeed, there were few conventional surfaces on which one could stencil. The wooden ceiling with its huge oak beams needed no more than a very thin pinkish whitewash to cool its tendency to appear orange, and the stone walls were also washed with this whitewash to moderate their darker khaki tones. There was one curved interior wall, screening the kitchen staircase, that was dappled with the colours of a sky, fading. On this wall I translated into stencilling bunches of herbs and dried flowers that hung from beams nearby.

In the centre of the room were hardwood sinks and work-tops, their plastered sides inset with drawers and shelves. These were painted just like a wall, pale blue-grey, strongly textured over with Indian red, and I designed a frieze of bronzed wheat which formed a horizontal banding around its base and top.

In this room the impact of the stencil was only gradually perceived, as details like the ears of wheat and a tawny red fox on the high back of a wooden chair emerged. At night, when eight dark-green shutters were pulled across the window, there appeared a line of golden oak leaves and acorns.

The central work unit, below, *ringed by wheat stencils,*   above right, *contains two wooden sinks.*

The treacly varnish already
on the chair, right, was a good
foil for the fox's natural
colouring.

To echo the green of a steep
grove of beech trees outside
the window, I introduced
dark-green shutters, bottom

left, green Wedgwood plates,
bottom right, and stencilled
bunches of bay leaves and
rosemary, above left.

I was drawn to the texture of surfaces with the quality of ageing about them. Old trunks for storage and practical blanket chests seemed particularly inviting surfaces for the imagination to feed on. One was masked with the strange, linear daubs of combed varnish; what particularly caught my eye were the floating lines on the front panel, curving like the underbelly of an animal. A taut young lioness, flanked by a pair of small palm trees, was the result of mulling over this provocative surface.

A large strongbox, bound about with iron strapping, received similar guard-like imagery. A threatening leopard sprawls across its front; another sits alert on one side, a cobra on the other. The top of the box is decorated with a spread of exotic fruit. The appeal of these designs draws upon the richness of their underlying texture.

The design on the lioness box, opposite, *makes careful use of the artificially grained wood beneath. The spots of the background to the cheetah,* above *and* below right, *counterbalance the animal's spots. The exotic fruits on the lid,* below left, *suggest pomegranates.*

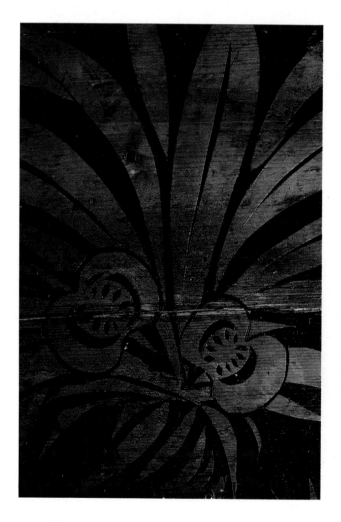

40

Wanting to design a floor decoration that would look like the carpet we could not afford, I studied books full of Eastern rugs, sketching, in particular, borders and blocks of pattern that might be suitable for a repeating stencil. I chose Indian red, indigo blue and yellow-ochre as colours that would work well with the yellow-beige of the boards and the grey-blue of the old bricks surrounding them. I then drew up in detail the design I had selected, measuring the floor exactly and working out the size I would need to make the stencils. The design was finally broken down into three separate stencils: an outsized tile shape, a chevron-border with a corner, and a small berried device for placing between each tile (this was also used to fill the gap where the chevron changed direction on the border).

The regular spacing of these stencils gives the impression that a carpet is laid over the brick floor, opposite. The colours reflect those of the cheetah box, below.

The Sitting-Room

We carved off one half of the big barn for a sitting-room, raising it three to four feet off the ground to make a large, shallow room. This meant that only two of the walls were formed from the original fabric of the old building. In order to give this complex some unity I devised stencilled panels on each wall; this broke up the surfaces, integrating and merging the old with the new.

I marked out these panels with a narrow, Paisley-like border in pink bronze on the strongly textured walls washed with a muted ochre colour. In addition, at each end of the mantelpiece were stencilled two formal urns containing fruit and corn. These completed the stencil-work and gave the whole room a

mellow, settled look (not unaided by wood smoke from the huge open fire), making it difficult to discern which walls were new and which were original.

It is perhaps a surprising fact, after the list of projects just recounted, that stencilling did not dominate the barn. Only gradually did one register that the plums on the pale-green cupboard doors in the garden studio were, in fact, stencilled. The little black boar with its pink tongue, stamped on the shield of a bit of old carving, was also made with a stencil. Even the fragmented rings of leaves on a cloth and makeshift canopy at a party were stencilled.

There was a restraint about it all that made the stencilling seem no more visually preoccupying than other patterned surfaces that go into refurbishing a house, such as textiles, wallpaper, carpets and china. And that is as it should be: rich, yet undemanding and peaceful.

Opposite above: *The border that forms the panels in this room was applied around the edges of the lampshades.* Above: *The interior of the garden room, used as a studio; a cupboard is stencilled with plums and cherries. The little boar, right, is from my husband's family crest.*

Left and opposite: *The colours of the geraniums ranged from scarlet to pink to white. I also reversed the stencil to simulate variety.*

STENCILLING FOR OTHERS

Wicker Walls in Stow-on-the-Wold

At about the time I was beginning to practise the art of stencilling, privately and sheltered in my own home, a friend showed me a sample of wallpaper she intended to use in her dining-room. This had a stamped-out design, a rather lukewarm imitation of early American stencilling. I was surprised and a little alarmed to hear myself boldly offering to hand-stencil the area for the price of the wallpaper. I don't know what I thought I was going to prove, but my rash impulse has served me in good stead!

The room was large, but one section of it had a lower ceiling, which seemed to divide it off naturally as an area in which to eat. My suggestion was to wicker-work the whole surface of this area and run a plaited frieze around the top (this would be continued through into the main room). Large stencilled pots of geraniums housed in arched alcoves were interspersed with the overall pattern. Although there was only one main stencil (reversed in alternate alcoves), the illusion of variety was created. Above a side-table, I stencilled the image of a fountain spurting water from a terracotta bowl filled with goldfish.

After this I found myself working for an increasing number of clients on a great diversity of commissions: private houses, hotels, clubs, shops and banks. In order to illustrate the wide variety of applications for stencilling and the effects that can be achieved, I shall describe a number of these projects.

An antique dealer, whose house had been put together with great style and panache, asked me to decorate her bathroom. The scale of this, however, was surprising – almost as if it were part of another house. My brief was to enhance the look of this room so that it matched the rest of the house.

My client's enthusiasm spilled over in all directions. She adored her house, in which she had been living since pre-war days, so I suggested that we should use the house itself as an image. The whole street could appear around the room, with her house as a cameo on one wall. She also loved Busy Lizzies (*Impatiens*) and the acacia trees in the street outside, so I used them to form an irregular wreath encircling the house.

Other elements brought into the design were some fragments of beautiful old cast-iron railings which I discovered in the garden; these made a lovely, rather formal frieze for the utilitarian pink bath and white tiles. Applied in a bronze-pink and brought close in around the tiles, this lifted the bath's colour and enlivened the white of the tiles, making the appearance of the room much smarter, as bordering always does. I put the same frieze around the top of the wall as the bathroom was quite small; this held the whole design together.

Some fine urns from outside were brought into play; two of these were set on high columns to serve as devices appearing to hold up the corners of the room and lending an air of architectural dignity. They contain plants with leaves curling over to enclose the corners of the ceiling.

Below left: Architectural details, like the fanlight,

panelling and doorknocker, were cut into the stencil.

A scaled-down version of the leafy fronds fills the miniature flower box, above.

Top: *Stencilling should not be treated too reverently – here a heater is attached to the wall over the stencilling.*

The original ironwork, above right, and columns, above, that were incorporated in the overall design.

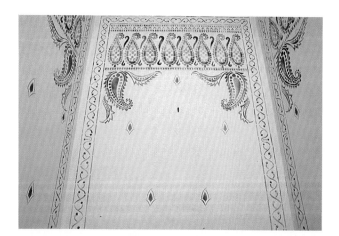

Another commission was the small cloakroom of a flat in central London, which needed to be brought alive. I decided that I could make this extremely ordinary interior into something that was very rich and textural, since it led off a smart hallway.

I took designs from some old cashmere shawls and used the elements to panel the room. I stencilled a very broad border at the bottom of the panel, a narrower one at the top. To this I added curly corner elements and then in-fills of a much simpler design. I gave the door the same treatment, so that when the door was closed it gave the impression of a sumptuously panelled room.

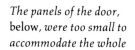

The panels of the door, below, were too small to accommodate the whole design, so the motif was stencilled into the outer corners only.

Above and opposite:
Repeating the design in each corner creates an intense concentration of pattern. A small spearhead motif fills in the field of the design.

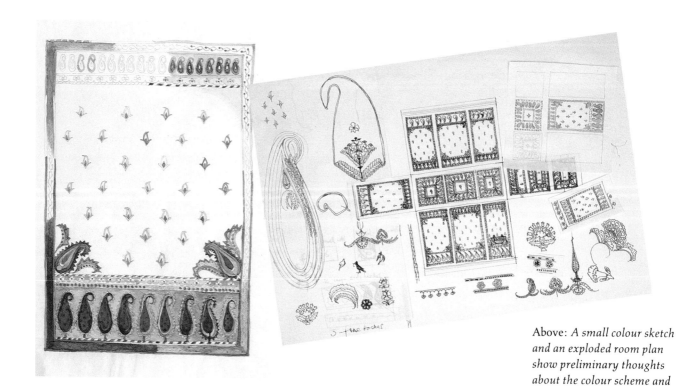

Above: *A small colour sketch and an exploded room plan show preliminary thoughts about the colour scheme and possible motifs.*

Because this is an interior room, opposite below, it was essential to use clear, light colours. The details right and below show how the colours blend together as you work, creating new shades altogether.

The Isle of Wight house
appears on these walls.

The corner of the room, top
and opposite, above, were
masked before I started work
to prevent blurring of the
stencilled image. The scene
depicts a point specked with
yachts, above; the house on
the skyline, above left, and
boathouse, left; and the path
to the water, opposite below.

Country Houses in Belgravia

This room is a small dining-room in a Regency house in Chester Row. I was called in to design a frieze to go around the top of the room in the traditional manner. This was the original idea but when the clients became further involved I was asked what I would do if I had a totally free hand. Having recently been inspired by the early American rooms where total landscapes – quite naive – were transferred courageously on to walls, I thought I might try this. It struck me as a glamorous background for a room in which people would be eating sociably together, perhaps by candlelight. When I put this to the clients they were enthusiastic and suggested I incorporate within the landscape places which were important to them as a family; a house in Rutland and a holiday home in the Isle of Wight. There was something rather intriguing about the idea of bringing the family's country houses into their London home.

I visited both places, making sketch drawings for

Whereas the rope-like border for the Isle of Wight scene appears nautical, here it is more formal, evoking the look of garden furniture, far left and bottom. Left: A crescent of lilac borders the house.

atmosphere and photographing specific details for more factual information. While the house in Rutland was of classical design, the one on the Isle of Wight was less formal architecturally and therefore less easy to translate into the stylized stencilled form. I felt that the best thing to do there was to go to the beach below the house, which had a strong romantic feel to it, and work from there looking up at the house. And so, after taking the long view, an offshore view of the property in its whole environment, it emerged with the feeling of a pavilion dominating a Japanese landscape, a much more amenable scene to stencil. In order to create the feeling of it being on an island, I included the two headlands at either end of the beach. In this rather complex manner I worked out a formal scheme for this building which would complement the classical style of the Rutland house.

Treating each wall as a canvas, I ran stencils of the two houses round the whole room. This commission showed that it is possible to represent a naturalistic scene with remarkable effectiveness, proving the tremendous versatility of the stencilling process.

*These panels show the
main house in Rutland,
below,* with its classical
details and garden borders,
opposite, far left, *and* right,
the pretty gatehouse.

I was asked to decorate the landing of an immensely beautiful house built in the Strawberry Hill-style in Warwickshire. The landing linked two grand staircases, forming a large room with six doors leading off it, the two main ones from the staircase at each end and a flanking pair at either side. There are no windows; the space is lit by a coloured glass dome.

The room had been known as the black-and-white landing and was said to have been always hurried through because it was thought to be haunted. My clients were eager to dispel its rather gloomy atmosphere and it was agreed to transform the whole into the illusion of an enormous hot-house. The revitalized area would be filled with the colours of exotic fruit and flowers.

This idea needed a visual structure, the elements for which I found in other Strawberry Hill-inspired houses, such as the Pineapple house belonging to the Landmark Trust. From this building I took details of

the windows, which I used as a backdrop to the stencilled plants and pots.

I made some drawings of the low parapets enclosing the formal gardens of the park and used these to produce a decorative balcony effect on which to stand the pots. This was placed immediately above the pine dado, beautifully marbled in putty-grey by Colefax & Fowler. To lend continuity as one walked into the room, I stencilled a very simple cornice design taken from a moulding on one of the staircases outside it. As the shapes of the landing doors were so excellent, I adorned them with a pineapple motif and, beside each door, stencilled a pair of stone pillars which supported potted palms.

In the decorative pots, I depicted mimosa, camellias, lilies, orange trees and hibiscus. In order to achieve a realistic effect, I was careful to keep the plants and pots in proportion to one another, cutting each as a whole stencil.

Opposite: *The exotic imagery of a hothouse helps to create an illusion of warmth and light.* Top: *The window stencil was carefully masked off where it was intersected by plant* stems and pots, and the more fragile mimosa sprays were simply stencilled on top. To break up the symmetry of the design, orange trees appear at different heights, *above.*

A Hillside Entrance Hall

I n this fine Gloucestershire house, I was commissioned to decorate a square entrance-hall, which was furnished as a room. As the whole of the house is very prettily furnished, my clients wanted the hall to have some impact on visitors, using imagery that would blend with the style of the rest of the house.

Around the top of the walls I stencilled a frieze with ribbons and leaves, from which hung bird-cages of various sizes; birds were also depicted flying freely round the room. Under the beams which interrupted the frieze, I slung a stencilled bunch of flowers, echoing those hanging along the top of the mirror over the mantelpiece.

A pretty little wood-burning stove had been placed in the very plainly plastered chimney-piece, which I stencilled to look as if it had a decorative moulding.

In the small outer porch there was an early mullioned window. Here I repeated the frieze which I had first designed for my own bedroom at Wells Head.

Just as the border drops to accommodate a structural beam, above left, so another variation is designed to go behind the chimney breast, opposite. Where damp dissolves salts in the plaster, bottom left, enjoy the texture that this creates. A similar border frames the pretty stove. The illusion of the rounded birdcage, left, is heightened by the curve of the wall, below.

The layout of the stencil work on this wall was carefully proportioned to be in balance with the portrait of the young boy, above. Below left: *The door with a leaning tree* and, below right, *a group of fireplace panels depicting wild flowers.*

An Indoor Garden in Wimbledon

When I was asked to stencil this drawing-room, my client was planning and planting her large garden. It seemed natural to extend her plans and turn this room into another sort of garden.

A parapet is stencilled to run squarely around the lower portion of the room, stopping each side of the window bay. Along this ledge flower-pots and urns are placed at intervals. An elegant pair of urns are carefully spaced each side of a family portrait; they contain spiky Dresina palms. At one side of these is a glossy Mexican orange-blossom bush and, at the other, a pot of delicately coloured orchids. A laburnum tree arches over the door; this is balanced in other corners by roses climbing to the ceiling.

A second pair of urns, with shallow dish-like bowls, hold grey-green succulents. There are more orchids around the mantelpiece, and a group of irises grow beside a low window. Flanking the main bay-window stand a tall pair of pyramid bay trees. Sprays of bay leaves are stencilled criss-crossing the base of the blinds and encircling the central light.

An illusion of airy space is created above the parapet; an illusion that is further enhanced when the room is candle-lit for supper parties.

Opposite, top: *A long, narrow chiffonier is usually placed symmetrically between the shallow urns.* Opposite, top right: *Blinds that tone with the curtains are sharply* stencilled with branches of bay leaves. Opposite, below: *Details of an orchid design, irises and the orange-blossom bush which tumbles over the balustrade.*

The main project in this house was the large kitchen in which the family could eat less formally than in their dining-room. They had a large, very beautiful, Chinese cabinet – a most unusual piece of furniture for a kitchen. My client set the stamp by saying that this impressive piece of furniture would obviously dominate the kitchen and she wanted everything worked around it.

From the Chinese cabinet I derived ideas for simulated tiling, which I stencilled behind the Aga cooker and between the work-tops and the higher cupboards. This tied these disparate elements together and made them architecturally more interesting.

For the mock tiles I used similar colouring. Some detailing on the tiles was based on that of the cupboard, where there was a bird hanging in a ring. The other motifs came from a piece of Chinese embroidery which I had always liked, and also a Chinese mug of mine which was painted with entwined fishes.

Although the tiles, opposite, *appear separate, in fact eight units are cut into each stencil. A device using a strip of plain tiles above the worktop (*above *and*

*opposite) and in the corners (*below right) *prevent the repeat from looking too mechanical. Below left: The Chinese cabinet that inspired the tile motifs.*

Opposite: *Dried pink and lavender flowers add gentle colours to a predominantly blue-green scheme.*

We decided to hang some stencilled herbs around the kitchen – strings of garlic, dried flowers, bay leaves above the cooker – generally to break up the vast surfaces of the room.

The client was very interested in china, and was indeed quite an expert. Showing me her very beautiful collection, she picked out a plate of which she was particularly fond, which had the family crest on it. We settled on the idea of designing a whole range of stencils of china decorated with this motif. I also included jugs, tea-caddies and fish-kettles, all on a grand scale. A high picture-rail was put in which simulated a plate-rail, and I stencilled the large pieces of china and other kitchen paraphernalia above this.

A compact border of twisted ribbon, *below left,* was stencilled on the plate-rail and around the stove alcove.

Above and below left: *Two plates and a tankard display the family crest. Below right: a large dish and fish kettle.*

As a source for the designs for a kitchen and breakfast-room in this house in Surrey, I used an original American quilt that the owners had brought back from the United States. This was extremely beautiful, worked in bottle-green and white cotton and appliquéd with baskets and vases of flowers in primary colours: egg-yellow, bright red, leaf-green and sky-blue. I used this theme not only to decorate all the panels of the newly fitted kitchen, which was large, but also to work out a serpentine frieze to go round the top of the walls, above the cupboards. We used a version of the frieze between the ceiling beams in the breakfast-room.

The stencilling had a traditional, early-American look, offset by a more modern colour scheme – walls in a clear and luminous pale pink, and the woodwork of the kitchen fitments stained and rubbed a sharp sap-green. This provided an astringent departure from the original colouring of the quilt.

The frieze that runs along the top of the cabinets, above *and* opposite, *was also applied between the ceiling beams in the breakfast-room, where the original quilt hangs,* below, far right. *Behind the cooker,* below left, *a stencil resembling a sampler was applied to the plaster. Several stencilled designs were cut to fit the shapes of the cupboard panels,* below centre *and* bottom right.

It is a great convenience of stencilling that you can tailor your design to fit existing architecture. The border, below, *was adapted to follow the sweeping curve of the banister,* opposite. Above:

The original carving on the riser. A single leaf design, above right, was applied at the intersections of the broken lines.

A Georgian Hall

In Hampstead, I was commissioned to stencil a group of adjoining floors in a Georgian house. The beautiful square hall was bordered on two sides by a fine old carved staircase and it seemed obvious to draw on the imagery that was already there on the carved supports of the stairs. I designed the border for the specially laid pine floor, working from the rustic rococo foliage of the stair supports. This was to run around the graceful circular end of the staircase and boldly edge the floor as a whole.

I drew heads of palm-like trees from the foliage and stencilled a broken criss-cross line representing stylized narrow trunks; these stretched across and divided the floor. They were joined by more foliage where they crossed, and within each of the squares thus formed was another scattering of leaves. The colouring of the leaves intensified the colours already present in the wood of the boards. As the house borders Hampstead Heath, the leafy imagery seemed particularly appropriate, as though dry leaves had blown in through the open door.

In the next room there were some Hockney drawings – the Los Angeles series. Here I developed the palm element rather more obviously. Using softer colours, I stencilled a border which ran alongside the brass edging holding the off-white Berber rug firmly in place. The leaves in the border tied in with the design in the hall on to which the room opened.

Opposite: *The brick-red border accent complements the flooring of the adjoining kitchen. A brass binding,* right *and* above, *holds the carpet firmly in place alongside the stencilled border.* Far right: *One of the Hockney drawings in the room.*

Cole Park

Here I was commissioned by Anouska Hempel to work on designs for some floors for her house in the country. I was given a large and very fine piece of Italian or French wood-carving, which still had traces of its original colour on its now-faded painted surface, and from this I worked out several schemes. The one finally chosen used the shapely rings on the carving to carry cloth curving through it. The colours of the carving were to be adapted, deepened to suit the tapestries that hung from the walls and lay across the bed. I had to work out a border linking my design

Design sheets, above, show a variety of proposals for this floor. A broad border of wood was mitred to meet the demands of the room, opposite. Groups of large individual fruits, below, are placed inside the wide border.

around the edge of the floor laid with wide oak boards, elegantly mitred at the corners. To carry the decoration across the entire floor, clusters of strange and robust fruit were stencilled at regular intervals.

My client also had the notion of turning the floor of her daughter's bedroom into a garden with flower-beds around a centrally paved area. Large pale petalled blooms were to be enclosed by the shell-like edging-bricks of the kind used to border Victorian cottage gardens; the flowers related to the Lillian Delavoryas fabric used in this room. This idea was extended to the passage, which became a paved walkway with flower-beds. The colours had to continue the very pale tones of all the furnishings of the top floor of the house, bleached and muted, but still varied within their restricted tonal range.

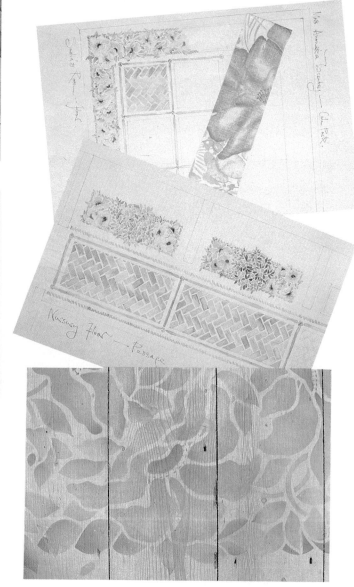

The floor of this nursery room and the passage leading to it were bordered with a faded rope and knotted ribbon, above. The pink ribbon also borders the walls. A large knot stencilled on either side of the threshold, top, imitates a hemp mat. Above right: Design sheets with a cutting of the curtain fabric that inspired the flowery floor stencil, right and opposite.

79

A t the time I was called to stencil at the Royal Crescent Hotel at Bath, great care and attention was being devoted to refurbishing it. The spectacular bedrooms, displaying meticulous attention to luxurious details, had been completed but, to my eye, the bathrooms adjoining them were a disappointment. Since one probably spends more hours awake and alert in the bath than in bed, this seemed a pity.

The space for these bathrooms has been ingeniously created throughout the hotel with minimum disruption to the classical shapes of the rooms, and when, after discussion, I was asked to go ahead with the decoration of some eleven bathrooms, I worked out three themes that took account of the changes in height and scale of the rooms on each floor.

For the bathrooms fitted with marble adjoining the grander rooms, I devised a form of Regency grotto, in which water splashes from a large shell down into a fish-pool fringed with ferns and lilies.

On the top floor the lower panes of the windows are masked by a stone balustrade which caps the entire stretch of this unique architectural crescent. I decided to utilize this balustrade as a device to create an illusion of space in the smaller bathrooms of this floor. Airy balconies are surmounted by stone urns filled with hydrangeas and daisy-trees, and I included butterflies to create a sense of being in the open.

For the bathrooms at garden level I brought in great Chinese pots, filled with plum and apricot trees, around which fly thieving birds. The coloured pattern on the pots varies from room to room; sometimes it is just china-blue and sometimes it is enhanced with a variety of richer colours.

Top: *The stencilling in the taller rooms on the first floor.* Above: *Smaller bathrooms tucked under the eaves on the top floor. The colouring of the pattern on the pots in the garden-level rooms,* below, *varies from room to room, as do the fruits, which may appear as apricots, greengages or plums,* opposite *and* below right.

In this hairdressing salon my first brief was to work on the ground floor, where the client said he wanted to create an atmosphere of luxuriant escapism; he had just returned from scuba diving in Barbados. I suggested using Gauguin and Matisse, artists who had painted powerful and exotic images, as sources for the scheme, and the client agreed. I decided to work in the first instance from some particularly apt Gauguin woodcuts, very strong in shape and form; they, interestingly, already had a broken-up, stencil-like feel to them. From these I progressed to imagery of my own invention.

The plan for the whole of the downstairs salon was to have a feeling of relaxing in a balcony of a house on one of these islands. The room upstairs was totally different, much lighter, and a year elapsed between the two parts of the commission. To link together the complicated room, I used water at different levels, swooping and dropping in waterfalls and making friezes at unusual levels on the walls, so that wher-ever the customers' eyes rested, they would see a new and arresting image. Even when customers are lying back with their heads in basins they can see water cascading with butterflies and humming birds hovering. In the men's salon, a tall, funnel-like space, I used native maidens in the columned manner of caryatids. Above them water swirls like a whirlpool before gushing down over their half-naked bodies.

In this room I applied friezes at unusual levels on the walls, opposite, far left, so that customers' eyes would be caught by fresh images on every side. Where a shelf occurs on a wall, the design is simply cut and continued in the space below, opposite, below left. The shapes of the maidens' sarongs provide generous areas for even more exotic patterns, above. Below and opposite: Sockets and lights are incorporated in the designs.

Crabtree and Evelyn

Crabtree and Evelyn are internationally known for their excellence of presentation. I was extremely interested therefore when they approached me to work on their shop in Kensington Church Street in London. I produced a number of visualizations for the treatment of the shop-front. Once the design had been chosen, it was not difficult to develop co-ordinated imagery for the whole shop, based on a complex motif of fruit intertwined with cloth.

It was challenging to work on the variety of surfaces involved: glass, cloth for the curtains, canvas for a garden canopy, painted marble for the exterior of the shop, stained panels and plaster friezes. The images themselves were adaptable to the changes of scale, particularly at the front of the shop where they

Design sketches, above right, show a variety of treatments for the front of the shop, opposite. *The stencilling on the columns flanking the door,* bottom left *and* opposite, *the underside of the arch and the blinds creates the effect of a garden trellis intertwined with ivy.* Below right: *A detail of the 'stonework' painted on glass.*

had to be enlarged. The stencil used for this was comparatively crude, but this was necessary for it to read in an external context. At the other extreme, the job also involved working with minute stencils on the dozens of small cupboard- and drawer-fronts. I was pleased with the decorated cloth of the large frieze, which I achieved by spraying the pattern through a second stencil on to the soft blue ground of the already stencilled basic material.

It would have been a tedious job to remove all the drawer pulls, above, so funnel-shaped hoods were slipped over them for protection.

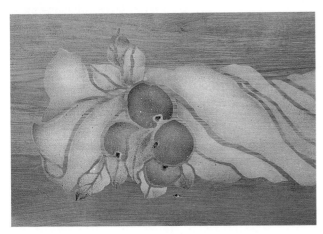

Opposite, below: *A patterned cloth frieze, decorated shelf panels and drawer fronts combine to make a harmonious whole with the closely stacked shelves. Because the grain of the wood* *introduces another texture to the stencilling, the twisted-cloth pattern on the shelf panels, right, was left plain. On the drawer fittings a frame with curved corners, below, imitates the moulding.*

Above and right: *The design used on the wooden panelling was stencilled on to the rough silk of the curtain material, then cut out to create ties. Individual leaves were appliquéd on top, and stuffed fruits, sprayed with fruity colours, were stitched in place. A big knot of fabric and bay leaves was devised to link the complicated ends of this border*, opposite below.

Quite early in my days as a stenciller I was presented with the fairly formidable task of decorating the walls of Regine's large London nightclub. My particular concern was with the restaurant area, which was to contain about thirty screens, each measuring nine by four feet. These were to have a continuous (albeit disconnected) design of cranes flying above golden clouds in a midnight-blue sky.

Another part of the commission was to work on designs for the cloakrooms. For these I designed two styles of chevron friezes, one with lilies, the other with palms. For the doors, which I consider the most successful part of the project, we were working on very plain marine plywood and were able – through the use of spray paint and a compact yet fragmented design – to achieve something of the appearance and richness of marquetry; this proved an interesting and effective way of transforming the surface of a fairly cheap material into something much richer.

The flying cranes on the screens of the main restaurant, top *and* above, *are reflected in the ceiling of mirrored tiles.* Opposite: *A chevron background with stars creates a frame for the fashion-plate looks of both the men's and the women's washrooms.*

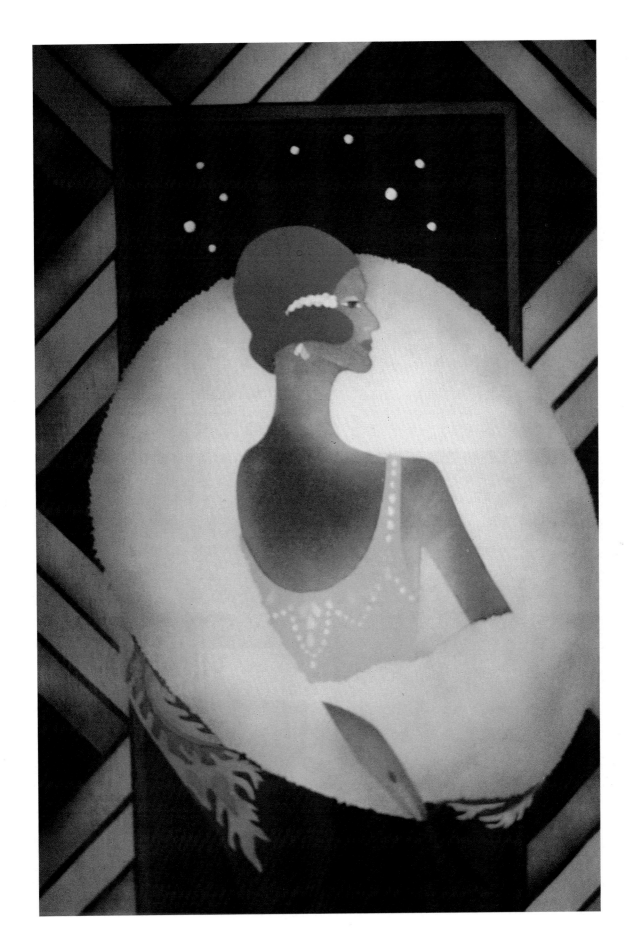

The restaurant of the elegant Blake's Hotel in London has an area where people can sit to have drinks when they first arrive. Here my commission was to work from the already positioned Chinese screen which ran along the length of one wall. The screen had six panels and was fixed above the terracotta-coloured seating which extended round the whole room. The wall behind the screen was painted black, setting off the strong, vivid colours of the screen to dramatic effect. I was to bring the same feeling of drama to the rest of the room.

I worked with perhaps the largest stencils I have ever made – and certainly the most complex. I cut a number of variations from the designs on the screen, assembling them into large panels somewhat wider than the panels of the screen itself. The composition had to be adjusted carefully to achieve the correct balance within the new panels. Around each panel I simulated the border design of the main screen, as

Above: *The crane in the centre of one of the panels.* Below: *One of the exotic birds in the top corner of the inner border, with details of the flowering tree in which it sits. The outer border of this panel,* below left *and* opposite, *with its change of scale, also acts as a frieze for the mirrored walls. To give strength, the thin lines framing the panels,* below right, *are spaced so that they do not coincide.*

well as using it as a frieze to link my panels to the screen itself in a rather strict, slightly Japanese, way.

When the whole room was stencilled, we lacquered the panels which I had made so that they matched the rich gleam and varnish of the original screen. The result is a richly patterned panelled room, a suitably glamorous setting for the clientele of this beautiful hotel.

Opposite: *The large bird in this panel perches above a luxuriant flowering lily. The spots in the fretwork design,* top, *were applied by hand with an opaque marker pen, as were the stamens in the centre of the pale-yellow blossoms,* top right *and* opposite.

95

Along the top of the screen is a boxed series of fans, top, their outlines sharply cutting through complete images. The stencilling was lacquered only to the panels' edges; the rest of the wall retained a matt finish, opposite.

97

STENCILLING MADE SIMPLE

Decorating an Old Cornish Mill

Pattern and decoration tend to emerge as necessary ingredients in man's lifestyle; even with the most impoverished communities time and means are found to satisfy this need – in Mexico, for example, where buildings are freely and exuberantly decorated in a manner that I prize: paint upon old paint, bright colours clinging to a surface in a fragile and transitory way, weathered thin with time. This is so refreshingly humane when compared with the manufactured surfaces that we are persuaded to live with today. The products of our high-tech society, synthe-tic paint, formica, plastic, and so on, provide no solace for me. As you have now seen, it is within the scope of stencilling to refresh and revitalize decoration, freely transforming many surfaces with imagery.

Before examining specific aspects of design and technique, it may be helpful to see the variety of ways in which you can distribute your stencilling within a room and to touch on other preliminary considerations. In order to do this I have designed a group of stencils that are commercially available and show how one can modify the complexity of designs.

Left: *Muslin curtains and cambric cushions are stencilled with images* from the 'Willow Pattern'. *Simulated tiles appear behind the cooker*, opposite.

In my house in Cornwall there is a series of interrelated kitchen rooms. I have decorated these and other parts of the house with my latest series of commercially available stencils. Here I have used the 'Willow Pattern' stencils to gain a variety of effects. There is a 'Fence' (the most versatile) to extend and use as a border for panels and friezes, two larger 'Pagoda' motifs, three other smaller elements, and the 'Willow Tree' itself.

The 'Fence' design forms a small panel above the wainscoting, above, to enclose an American Seth Thomas wall clock. Top: The cameo shape created by the borders is filled with the sampan stencil that also appears on the curtains, above right, strung on dressmaker's tape for a simpler look. Opposite: The blue is echoed in the plates. Because the utility room is floored in slate, the kitchen linoleum was painted to look like stone tiles; a floral stencil breaks up the design, right.

The Dairy

In the dairy the small 'Pavilion' is applied in a plain and stamped-out manner on the old whitewashed walls. The spacing is wide and not strictly regular, and this emphasizes the quality of the undulating wall surface. The 'Pair of Birds' is fitted neatly into a square, tile-like framework in the utility room. The stencilling here has a waterproof coat of varnish and produces what are, in effect, tiles around the sink. These simulated tiles also protect the wall behind the Aga cooker.

The larger 'Pagoda' design was reversed on the cupboard doors, opposite, above. *The colouring of the tiles,* opposite, below, *blends with the old slate sink top.*

102

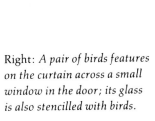

Right: *A pair of birds features on the curtain across a small window in the door; its glass is also stencilled with birds.*

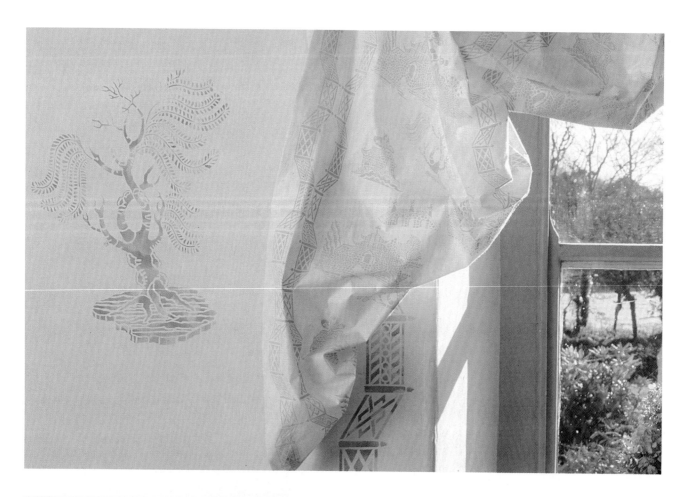

The Kitchen Rooms

Within this group of rooms, with their linking theme of 'Willow Pattern' stencils, I used a variety of treatments when it came to curtains.

In the breakfast-room glazed cambric printed with an all-over pattern is looped over poles fixed high above the windows. The curtains are finished with bows of stencilled stripes, tucked behind the small flowerheads of old metal brackets (opposite and left), which we sprayed with soft blues to match the stencilled pattern.

The simple muslin blocked with one stencil in a single colour, which was chosen for the kitchen, dairy and utility room, was hung in various ways. For example, a square of handkerchief-sized muslin, stencilled with birds, buttons over the small window in a door (see p. 103), while a pair of larger curtains, stencilled with boats, hangs across another door (see p. 100). Frame-like shutters were made for one window and infilled by muslin printed with the 'Bridge' design (see p. 98).

104

In the breakfast-room, below, the walls are panelled out more formally with the 'Fence', each of the larger motifs being placed centrally within a carefully scaled panel. This effect imposes a distinctive architectural framework on an otherwise ordinary room. The wainscot is a much larger variant of the 'Fence' design.

The detail of the 'Pagoda' *subtly blend. The curtains,*
stencil, opposite, above, *shows* above *and* below, *draw*
how the sprayed colours *together all the motifs.*

I bought a beautiful linen tablecloth and stencilled it with the blues of the 'Willow Pattern', opposite, forming an octagonal centrepiece with the 'Fence' design. The linen napkins, below, bore one of the smaller images.

Above: *The 'Fence' design on three different scales.*

The Little Parlour

In the small parlour off the kitchen the colouring is pale and muted. Panels are painted in soft grey-green, and the central one is stencilled with a pair of the 'Golden Pheasants'. The walls are dappled with paint the colour of calico, then stencilled with the narrow leaf border. Below this I painted a crude, simple type of panelling, which, while cutting this tiny room in half horizontally, oddly creates a feeling of space. Overtly pretty curtains and cushions carry the same stencilled design as the panels.

The bare boards of the floor were washed over with a coat of very dilute eau-de-nil emulsion paint, which softened their colour. The tufted border was stencilled as an edging following the room's irregularities.

Opposite: The pair of pheasants above the fireplace were originally stencilled in yellow ochre; later, finding the colour a bit timid, I over-stencilled with darker tones, above. The border that runs along the edge of the window-seat cushion, right, also forms panels on the walls.

My Bedroom and Bathroom

I designed the 'Cornish Thrift' set of stencils particularly for this bedroom (for pattern see pp. 157–159). The bronze-pink flowerheads and plants are scattered evenly across the walls, each of which is then edged with an unfolding 'Ribbon' border.

The gently broken texture of the walls is important in creating an appropriately sensitive background for this kind of low-key stencilling. It is achieved very simply here by means of some judicious neglect in preparing the walls for painting. Bedroom colours of soft pinks and blues, chosen by previous occupants, were left adhering to the walls. A thin coat of old-fashioned white distemper wash was brushed across the whole surface, making it softly translucent – particularly beautiful when struck obliquely by the

The fabric next to the bed, below, is embroidered with flower patterns in a manner not unlike stencilling. When objects are placed in front of stencilling, right, the effect is often intensified rather than obscured.

morning sun. With the pure white of linen curtaining hanging against this wall it appears quite coloured and mellow. The oak bed-panelling has had its linenfold sections whitened deliberately to form a visual link with the actual folds of the curtain linen hanging beside it. The painted woodwork is pale greenish-grey, complementing the subtle interwoven colours of Susan Marshall's printed rag rugs, which are also predominantly grey. A small alcove has been contrived with curving shelves to display some sponged and stencilled china.

In the bathroom leading off the 'Thrift' bedroom (shown in detail on p. 117) the stencils are applied to the panels of the linen cupboard and bath. As in the bedroom, I used several 'Thrift' designs on the cupboard panels, reversing them for greater variety. Brighter shades of pink, green and ochre were used here to compete with the stronger blues of the panels. A pale frieze rings the top of the room, a very muted version of the 'Ribbon Border'. The floor is paved off into diagonal stencilled lozenges in the same pale tones of grey and pink.

A clump of 'Thrift', as it appears in the bedroom, above, and on the end of the bath, opposite, below right. Where there is only a narrow field between two borders, a small flower head is stencilled, opposite, above left. The same small flower is used on walls generally, opposite, below right, and below, to link larger motifs.

Top: *In the recessed cupboard beside the fireplace,
the walls were painted a
rough but pretty blue and
stencilled with just the small
flower head.*

Above and opposite: The pattern on the floor was created by stencils and long strips of masking tape, which produced the diagonal lines. Because the colouring of the cupboard, below, provides a darker background for the 'Thrift' stencil, the softer hues used in the bedroom were exchanged for brighter greens, pinks and yellows.

STENCILLING FROM THE BEGINNING

Now that you have seen the richness and variety of effects that can be achieved by stencilling, it is time to explain the practical side of the craft so that you can try it for yourself. Do not be put off by the scale and apparent complexity of much of my work – the most intricate of designs are often made up from a number of simple individual motifs repeated to form a more complicated pattern. This is one of the joys of stencilling; you do not have to be an artist to produce an 'artistic' effect – anyone can draw (or trace) a simple motif which the stencilling process itself will transform into an attractive and memorable image. In this section the stencil process is fully described, including guidelines for design. There is information about the variety of surfaces one can stencil, the different techniques needed and the finishes which can then be applied. In the following chapter I go into a variety of projects you might like to try, with practical details regarding their execution. I have illustrated this last section with further examples of my own work to show what can be done.

SOURCES OF IMAGERY

When thinking of images to use for stencilling it is instructive to look very carefully at the ways in which people have decorated objects in the past, not for the purpose of slavish reproduction – for the greater satisfaction is usually gained from ideas you contribute yourself – but to discover the variety of subjects that have been used over the ages, and how these have been translated into design.

Even the grandest of decorative motifs are of familiar and personal subjects. Flowers, fruit and birds are particularly constant and much-loved themes, appearing repeatedly under different guises and in a variety of structural forms. Look, for example, at the richly decorated plasterwork and wood-carving of stately homes, at the sculpture and stained glass of churches and cathedrals, or the beautifully executed imagery of medieval manuscripts and books. Porcelain, carpets, antique textiles, embroideries and tapestry also provide invaluable sources of imagery for stencil work.

Notice, in many of these examples, how certain modifications are made necessary by changes in scale. The exotic peacock has been used in the past by decorators to embellish vast walls, their tails trailing or in display, but the feathery eye only may be picked out and used in repetition around the curve of a border on an elegant table. Similarly, while many garlands of flowers are used to form a continuous chain in some elaborately moulded plaster frieze, a single flower-head is enough to decorate the lid of a powder-box. You will often find these changes of scale are necessary when you translate an image on to your stencil card.

Look too at our rich outdoor heritage for sources of imagery: elaborate gateways, statues, fountains and the urns found in formal gardens present us with complex profiles, well suited to being cut into stencils, classical and lasting in their appeal. The image of a large and magnificent Versailles tub containing a fruiting orange tree might be stencilled beside the door of an entrance hall, or repeated to create an interior garden room softened with foliage. The very layout of gardens is rich in potential imagery; the ornate brickwork of paths, avenued drives and the formal, colourful scrolls of Palladian parterres, or the earlier, more intimate design of the Knot garden, with its patches of herbs and topiary of yew or box, present suitably evocative symbols of well-being.

Flowers offer themselves most aptly as subjects for stencil work. The variety in the structural formation of plants lends itself well to being broken up into segmented shapes: leaves, stems, petals and stamens. All of this suggests a particularly good area in which to look for imagery suitable for stencilling. The range is immense, from highly cultivated hot-house blooms – orchids or lilies – right through to wild flowers such as the modest dog-rose. Their appeal is far-reaching; few people fail to respond with warmth when asked to name their favourite flowers.

In your search for imagery, you might also turn to the animal world, in which case observing first-hand and drawing from life is not always easy. Some of the most useful sources of reference are children's books, where you will find animals and birds of all kinds lovingly recorded, often with a simplicity which makes them especially suitable for stencilling. Children's love of animals makes them favourite images for the stencilled high-chair or nursery wall.

In addition to natural symbols and motifs, there is a whole galaxy of shapes and patterns that are plain and geometric in form, the Greek key pattern being one of the simplest and most familiar. Combinations of straightforward squares, circles, triangles and lines, as well as more complex forms, are placed together and built up into patterns. Intricate, rich textures are compiled from small fragmented shapes, as in mosaic borders. Sticky coloured cut-out shapes for children can be used to assemble designs similar to those viewed through a kaleidoscope. Examples of abstract decoration can be seen on Islamic ceramics and pottery, Oriental rugs and many primitive artefacts as well as the tiled floors of cathedrals, palaces and public buildings.

These, then, are just some of the sources of the imagery I use in my stencil-work. There is inspiration all around us in the things we take for granted in everyday life, as well as in the objects we seek out to admire and imitate. But you may already have a definite idea of the image you wish to create by stencilling. If so, you are ready to start to learn how to translate your idea into reality.

DRAWING UP YOUR DESIGN

Having chosen your subject, begin by making some sketch notes, if possible directly from the subject, observing character closely; details as small as the stamens of a flower can often form important elements in design. Having made some sketches, begin to work them into a design idea for your stencilling.

Do not be inhibited by any shortcomings you may feel regarding your ability to draw. Be brave, and remember that the process itself has a habit of improving its own quality, over and above the drawing – a hidden bonus with stencilling.

If you find drawing from an object difficult you may find photographs will help, since the flattening of the image makes a shape easier to define and copy. It can also be helpful to look at drawings that others have made of the same subject and what details they have recorded. You can even trace a subject if you

I have a board on which I keep
postcards, photographs and
bits of fabric – snippets of

visual imagery that I like and
that may give me ideas for my
work. Cover a piece of soft

board with green baize and
criss-cross this with ribbon
to construct a grid that will

hold in place the things you
collect as inspirations for your
own designs.

like. Drawings made from tracings tend to be rather static but this is not necessarily an alien quality to stencil work. As a last resort you can even draw around the outline of an object (such as a leaf, for instance) found in a great variety of shapes and sizes.

The most successful stencilling has a powerful rhythmic quality. To achieve this, gradually flatten out areas for a two-dimensional effect, developing and emphasizing particular recurring shapes and features. Simple and effective patterns are made by repeating an uncomplicated shape to make a motif

and then repeating the motif to form a pattern or border.

Pattern can also be achieved by the grouping of subjects so that the repetition of shape in itself creates the design. More complex borders can be made up by simply repeating the same motif in a line and linking them with a complementary motif: if bunches of flowers are the motif they may be connected with such devices as trailing stems, leaves or meandering ribbons. Birds and butterflies can be linked rhythmically by the proximity of their wing tips.

Bordered
Panelled
Bedroom at
Thrift – sea pinks
Pale
broken walls
bronze/grey
leaves
sugar
pink
flower head
ribbon

BLOCKING IN, AND 'BRIDGES'

In order to demonstrate how to design and use a stencil, I have chosen the 'Thrift' and border stencils for my bedroom in our Cornish mill. Opposite is my working drawing for these. First I made simplified drawings from the plant, sketching its line and shape (opposite and top right). Below (centre) you see me working at the drawing, designing the detail of the flowerheads and the grass-like leaves, flattening and broadening them to create shapes that can be cut out as a flat pattern. In the same way, I tried out different designs for the ribbon.

Having worked out a possible design, you must clarify the areas that will need to be cut away to make the stencil. Block these in clearly with cross-hatching to make distinction easier. Remember that your final design will be formed only by the cross-hatched areas that are to be removed. When blocking, it is necessary to leave intact linking pieces as integral parts of the design. These bridge-like links hold the stencil together in one piece by connecting all parts of the design to the main body of the stencil after it is cut. (See the pictures on p. 125, which show clearly the card that is left between strips that have been cut away.)

Bridges should recur at regular intervals, otherwise the stencil could be endangered, its structure too weak to handle without breaking. Try to find ways of doing this so that the rhythm and vigour of the design are not halted. For instance, it will be necessary to break up the length of a long, flowing line such as a ribbon. By using a regular diagonal slant, the flow of the line is maintained. When planning the number and width of these bridges, always take into account the amount of design to be cut away. A complicated and dense design, in which much of the main body of the card is removed, must be balanced by plenty of bridges.

Although there is no standard width for the bridges, the larger the stencil, the heavier it is, and it will therefore require correspondingly wider bridges

for greater strength. There is, however, a limit to how narrowly they can be cut without becoming too fragile to withstand the physical manoeuvring involved in stencilling. They should be of uniform width in order to establish the rhythms that are so much part of the fluent stencilled image.

DRAWING UP THE STENCIL

You are now ready to transfer your design on to a piece of stencil-card. Manila card, soaked in linseed oil, makes the best stencils, since it is both substantial and tough, while also remaining pliable and easy to cut.

Work out the size of card you will need in relation to your design and the area or object you want to decorate. If the stencil-card is too small for the size of your design, join two pieces together and seal any necessary joins with masking-tape, pressed down flat on both sides. Remember also that it is very important that a 'frame' is left intact around the entire outside edge of the card to hold the whole stencil together. Mark off an area of 'no man's land' to remain uncut. From your drawing, map out the design on the stencil-card in pencil. Clarify the design using a dark fibre-tipped pen, as it shows up well and flows easily on the card's oily surface. Block in the shapes that you are to cut away as you did on the original drawing. As you gain confidence you may find that you can draw straight on to the stencil-card intuitively.

If your drawing needs to be enlarged, a foolproof way to do this is to draw a grid over your original sketch. This could be made up of, say, one-inch squares. To double the size, for example, measure out on your stencil-card the appropriate enlarged grid, that is, with the same number and order of *two*-inch squares. Transfer the contents of each small square to its corresponding one on the enlarged grid. If you concentrate on each square separately you will find the whole thing suddenly falls together, rather like the pieces of a puzzle. However, if you have access to a photocopier, you can simply use this to enlarge your design.

CUTTING THE STENCIL

You now need to cut away your blocked-in shapes, and for this you will need a good craft knife (or matte knife).

Cutting into the linseed-treated manila with a sharp, new blade is a pleasant task; there is no grain to cut against and the oiliness smooths your path. (However, if you are not finding this part of the process enjoyable, you are using too much pressure. Relax your shoulder and elbow and work from your wrist only.) By applying an even pressure it is possible to cut very fluently, and you can eventually learn to make lively improvements to the blocked-in shapes with a certain degree of virtuosity as you become more practised. Start from the middle of the design; in this way the maximum strength of the card is retained as you work. For the same reason it is a good idea to cut out the smaller shapes before the larger ones. Cut along the outer edge of the blocked-in areas so as to retain the clearest interpretation of the design. Manoeuvre the stencil so that you are always able to draw the knife towards you even when cutting round the smaller shapes. In this way small shapes, such as dots, can be cut in two easy movements. If you make a slip in cutting, take a narrow strip cut from a piece of masking-tape and seal the card on both sides, taking care to ensure that no tape protrudes over the cut edge of the design.

Cutting-boards, ideal for stencil-making, are available; these are 'self healing', closing up cut lines as you lift the knife away so that no ridges are left, even after prolonged use. Their bright-green colour shows up slack corners and badly cut curves, and their white lines assist with accurate straight lines. It is also, of course, possible to cut stencils with a piece of hardboard underneath for protection, but beware of cutting straight through on to a good table-top.

BORDER REPEATS

All borders incorporate a repeating motif. When repositioning a stencil again and again around walls or doors, it is essential to reproduce a continuous motif accurately. To do this you must ensure that the right-hand end of the stencil will meet, and fluently continue, the left-hand end. Draw a length of border design on stencil-card, leaving several inches of blank card at either end. Cut out the design. Now bend the card round to form a loop, and slide one end under the other until enough of the design can be seen through the outer layer of card to establish its flow. Using

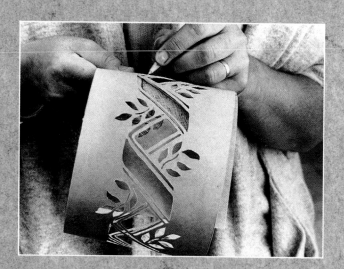

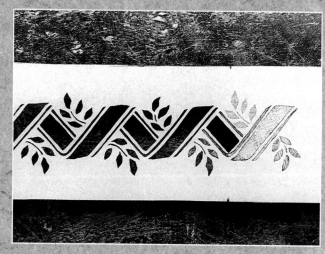

the holes in this outer layer as a guide, draw in the linking shapes, then unwind the card and cut them out.

BORDER CORNER-PIECES

When stencilling a border, you will need to design a corner-piece to link horizontal stretches with vertical ones. In order to draw up a corner-piece that joins the border accurately and fluently, first measure the *width* of the cut border design – the *length* of the stencil is not important (see 'Link-pieces' below). Then take a square piece of card and draw two right-angles, an inner and an outer, that form a 'frame' exactly the width of the border pattern. Leaving the corner itself blank, place your cut border stencil within the 'frame' on either side of the corner and draw or spray enough of the pattern to allow you to design a central corner motif that will link the border on both sides.

LINK-PIECES

The design of your frieze or border design may well not repeat an exact number of times across the surface you are to decorate. A link-piece will have to be cut to accommodate the discrepancy. The size of this piece is most accurately arrived at by fixing a good length of card across the remaining space and spraying over each end of it with the stencil in place on either side. Design the link-piece in the same way as the corner-piece. Measure the length of the gap, and adjust your frieze design to this final space.

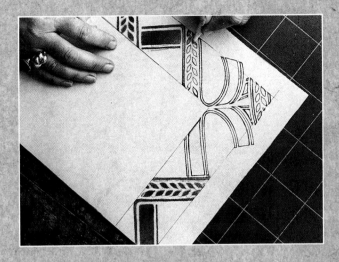

A SAFETY NOTE

I describe below techniques that may require the use of spray paints and adhesives. Whenever you use aerosol cans, follow the manufacturer's instructions meticulously. You should also take the following general precautions. (1) Ventilate as well as possible the room in which you are working. (2) Avoid breathing in the spray – a light face mask will serve as protection against this. (3) Wear goggles to safeguard your eyes, and suitable clothing to protect your hands and other exposed patches of skin. (4) *Do not smoke*: the content of most aerosol cans is flammable. If you are pregnant, it may be wise to avoid using aerosols altogether.

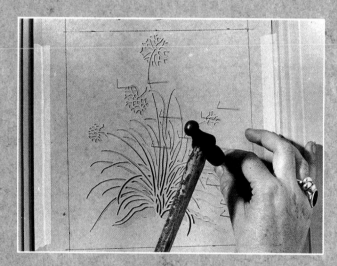

ATTACHING THE STENCIL

You have now cut out your stencil and wish to try it out. Before you start to stencil you must first ensure that all the edges of the design can be kept in close contact with the surface which you wish to stencil. This is to stop your paint seeping under the edges and spoiling the clean outline of your design. The fine spray of spray paint, for example, will drift under the smallest part of a loosely attached edge, so great care must be taken at this stage. A beautifully designed stencil can easily be blurred and spoilt by hurrying.

I have found that the most effective way of attaching stencils is to use an aerosol adhesive, generally available in larger graphics- and art-supply shops, which coats the surface with a thin layer of light adhesive that remains tacky for some time. The stencil can therefore be stuck down and lifted off a surface a number of times without damage to that surface. This works as well on fabrics as it does on other surfaces.

Place the stencil, reverse side up, on a sheet of newspaper and spray the glue thinly and evenly all over it. This process is easier if done against a vertical surface such as a door, since this prevents the nozzle clogging. Let it set for a few moments. When you are

ready, position the stencil accurately, glued side down, on the surface you are to decorate.

Some people may prefer to attach the stencil with dress-making pins: they take more time, but are far cheaper and, perhaps, more readily to hand. Tap them in with a small hammer at intervals along the cut edge of the design; they should only be inserted to the point at which they will stand firmly without support and can be pulled out easily with your fingers.

If you have chosen to work on metal, small bits of Blu-Tack re-usable adhesive or double-sided tape, applied sporadically to the underside of the stencil at regular intervals, are alternatives to aerosol adhesive. They will hold a stencil close to the surface when pressed down evenly and firmly.

Before attaching the stencil, you may have to cut its surround in places so that it can lie flat around any protuberances, such as handles, raised panels, locks, etc. Seal well around these cuts with masking-tape.

Having chosen your method of attachment, fix the position of the stencil with small strips of masking-tape to ensure that it does not shift during the stencilling process. Now protect the surface around the stencil with plenty of lining-paper, fixing it down firmly on to the edge with long strips of masking-tape, to prevent the spray from drifting underneath.

SPRAY COLOUR

I was delighted to discover the happy combination of spray paint in conjunction with stencils very early on, and have never felt the need to use any other medium for the job. By comparison, the traditional stubby stencil brush is a clumsy tool, and I find spray paint has a subtle versatility which this brush cannot provide. Spraying enables paint to be applied with the minimum of contact with the stencil at what would otherwise be a vulnerable stage of the operation. Use the push-button cans of aerosol paint which are primarily for matching and repairing paintwork on cars. The acrylic lacquer adheres powerfully to most

surfaces, giving a hard and durable finish; the colour does not fade; and the choice of colours is immense. There are also colours that have a metallic quality which, when used discreetly, add a gleaming lustre. Colours to imitate nature abound; greens range from conifer to palest willow, blues from high summer skies to stormy petrel-grey, reds from fiery scarlets to sand-, earth- and bark-brown. While the hard edge and solid primary colours of East European stencilling are possible with spraying, a fine spray allows a subtler, more sensitive look to emerge with the overlapping of one colour on another, which gives a mellow and gentle quality. I mix and blend my colours directly on to the surface that I am working on, at times using as many as five colours on a single leaf. There is no need to be timid with colour; it can be a source of much pleasure, fulfilling a naive and primitive need.

APPLYING SPRAY PAINT

When you have cut your stencil, it is a good idea to test it on paper first in case you want to modify it. You will also want to test your spray technique and your colours. Lining-paper is cheap and expendable for this and also useful to have nearby when testing out a new can or fresh colour.

I have found that I instinctively use a gentle pumping movement on the button, which produces a light sporadic spray. When you feel at ease with the spray button and have control over the direction and amount of spray leaving the nozzle, work out the best distance to hold the can from the area or object you are to decorate. This is generally three to six inches, but varies according to the size of area to be covered: hold it closer for small details and further away for larger, more expansive areas. From whatever distance you are spraying, it is important to avoid a sudden burst of paint building up in one spot, a result of holding the can too near, or clogging in the nozzle. If the paint runs, you are spraying too hard.

When working with different colours you can, if you choose, restrict each colour to within particular shapes by using a strip of stencil card two to four inches wide, held in your free hand while you spray. You will quickly learn to manipulate this 'guard', curving it adeptly around outer edges of the shapes with your fingers so that only those parts that you wish to colour are touched by the spray paint.

For very small details cut a hole in a spare piece of stencil-card, so that when you place this on your stencil only the detail to be sprayed is left showing through. If the detail is too small even for this, squirt a shot of colour into the lid of the can and use a fine brush to touch in the detail. Keep this touching-in to a bare minimum, however, so as not to interfere with the rhythm of the stencilling.

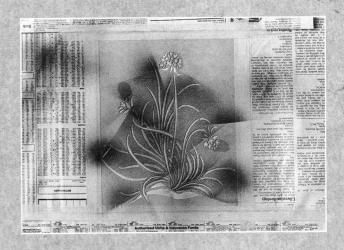

When spraying, almost the only mistake you can make is to spray too strongly. I use thin layers of spray, building up the colour slowly, allowing brief pauses for drying. For achieving solid colour the principle 'little and often' is still the best. However, solid blocks of colour need not be your overall aim; faintly applied paint can leave a surprisingly vivid impression when the stencil is lifted away. It is a mistake to think that colour has to be thick and strong to be effective.

I find that the combination of faintly and densely coloured areas produces an effect that is surprisingly three-dimensional, a quality not often associated with stencilling, which usually presents a blander, flatter face. But be careful to use this effect with restraint, or your stencilling may have the facile look of some rather slick airbrush work. The other real innovation of spray-stencilling lies in the subtle overall blending of colour, as when the rose-red from one side of an apple faintly tints the top of an adjoining leaf, with added advantage to both (as opposed to the painting in of individual shapes). This changes the emphasis of the stencilling from a more or less literal translation of particular objects and carries it on into the area of more sophisticated and evocative impressions.

The quick-drying properties of the spray paint – it has already begun to dry on leaving the can – cut down on the danger of smudging and allow the stencil to be removed almost at once, just when one is most eager to see results. When a stencil is repeated along a frieze or border there is no waiting around for the last print to dry before starting on the next alongside it.

STENCILLING A ROOM

Having followed through the design and cut and sprayed the 'Thrift' stencils, I describe here how they are applied to the wall of a room, using my bedroom as an example. Overleaf is a close-up of one wall, showing the border and individual 'Thrift' designs in place. A simple frieze was used on the walls of the bathroom with the 'Cornish Thrift' design on the panels of the cupboard and bath. In the bedroom a border runs up and around each wall area and over the doors, and the area thus enclosed is sparsely marked out with tufts of thrift. Before starting to stencil, the walls have been delicately prepared. The spray-stencilled image sits more happily on a surface that is not flat colour. In order to break up this colour, one can apply a dappling of a different tone. I often apply several different shades of colour to a wall to achieve a subtle tonal effect into which the stencilling will blend.

SIMPLE FRIEZE

We start with the straightforward frieze which encloses the space. Measure the depth you want the frieze to be from the ceiling. The distance from the top edge of the design to the edge of the card should be the same. You may have to trim the stencil frame or add an extra piece to the card. This will give you a consistent depth guide. Start in the corner nearest the main door in the room and work round this point.

When you get to corners mask them off vertically with a strip of masking tape. Place the stencil over this and fold it tightly into and round the corner. The masking tape, when pulled off, leaves the corner clean, preventing a blurring of the image. The break in the frieze blends with the characteristic breaking of the stencil. For an example of this, turn to the illustration on p. 88, showing corner junctions of the frieze for Crabtree and Evelyn.

BORDERING, USING CORNERS

Whole walls, as well as features such as doors and windows, can be bordered. For this the corner-piece is

necessary. Measure the distance of the border from the edge you are skirting, and adjust the edge of your corner stencils to coincide with this, as you did for the frieze. Start by stencilling in the corner piece. Now link up in each direction with the straight frieze stencil. It may be necessary to make new link-pieces to join the frieze where it meets in the centre.

You can use a frieze to break up the walls of your room into panelled areas. I have done this on the walls of my breakfast-room in Cornwall, illustrated on p. 106. This simple device is a most effective way of giving elegance to an otherwise banal room. For horizontal lines, measure from ceiling and skirting board. Mark out vertical lines, measuring from the corners, and mark the walls with a piece of tape,

putting an arrow on the tape to indicate which side you are measuring from. If there are any protuberances you cannot or do not wish to remove, such as handles, raised panels, light switches, you will have to cut the stencil in places to allow it to lie flat before attaching it. Seal around the cuts with masking tape.

POSITIONING A SINGLE MOTIF

To find the centre of your wall fix a pin into each corner of the wall and stretch two pieces of string diagonally from corner to corner. Mark the point at which these cross as the centre of your wall with a piece of masking tape. You can now position your

motifs in relation to these points. The centre of any area can be worked out in this way. In the finished room you will see the variety of ways a series of stencils has been used in order to create a cohesive look. Several groups of 'Thrift' were used as well as separate flower-heads to create this balance.

The completed walls were given a coat of water-glaze more as a protection for the wall than for the stencilling, which is itself tough and durable. The glaze is milky when applied but dries to a transparent finish. Be careful that this covering is total, since an area which is missed will discolour in relation to the whole.

DUPLICATING YOUR STENCIL

If a stencil is to be used a great many times, it is worth making a duplicate copy before you start stencilling, because eventually edges may begin to suffer from a build-up of paint, or it may get damaged with frequent handling. After testing to see if you are happy with it, make the duplicate. This is simply done; just lay out your stencil-card and spray the image through clearly with a dark-coloured paint. Only go on to cut out the design, however, when you are sure you will need it; the copy can act, in any case, as a conveniently strong mount on which to store your stencil when you have finished using it.

CLEANING UP

There is no need to clean a stencil after use, but it should be left in the open for twenty-four hours or so to allow any build-up of paint to dry completely; also a light dusting of talc can be applied to absorb any surplus glue left on stencils. Spray paint can be cleaned from hands with nail-varnish remover. Lighter fuel lifts away any small particles of adhesive left on the stencilled surface after the stencil is taken off, without harming the paint.

STENCILLING FOR YOURSELF

In this section I give more specific detail about the possibilities for stencilling different sorts of furniture and fabrics, and I describe some projects I have worked on. I have deliberately peppered this section with ideas for design imagery in the hope that you too may feel enthused and confident enough to tackle and transform a piece of furniture of your own.

FURNITURE

Stencilling may be carried out on a variety of painted surfaces: egg-shell, gloss or softer-textured emulsion (this requires a final protective coat of clear varnish). You can apply your paint in the usual way – primer, undercoat and top coat – or use two blending colours one after another and rub them down with fine sandpaper so that each colour shows on the surface in different places. Rub harder at corners and edges, which would have been naturally worn. This technique adds a mellow richness to the surface that complements the finished stencilling. Different textures may be achieved by applying the final coat of paint with a rag, sponge or upheld brush, again letting the first colour show through.

Polishing gives a satisfying finish to stencilling, integrating it well with the surface and at the same time picking out areas of colour which reflect light. Polish can be applied after twenty-four hours.

BOXES AND CHESTS

A wooden box or chest offers simple, flat and unfettered surfaces, and its scale, which is not too daunting, makes it a good first object for stencilling. By working first on an old tool chest, I was taking no risk whatsoever. It was the colour of its rough painted surface, a soft grey-green, that appealed to me. I stencilled directly on to this old surface after giving it a good clean with soap and water. If the original paint on your box is a good colour and texture, you may choose to retain it. If, however, the paint on your box

is cracked or badly applied, or you do not like the colour, strip it back to the wood and start afresh. Take care with paint remover; harshly stripped wood offers a texture little better than strawboard.

Check the existing lock, handles, hinges or metal strapping. They will probably not need to be replaced, but they should function. Clearing a paint-clogged lock or oiling hinges is simple at this stage but can make a mess of your paintwork later.

Your design will probably dictate the surface colour. However, traditional background colours for country furniture were lamp-black, Indian red, Sienna, dark green and a chalky French blue; these were the cheapest and most readily available as they were made from natural substances.

Look at the inside of the box carefully. It might be worth relining it with cloth or pretty paper, or you might perhaps consider stencilling this in keeping with the outside. You may choose to introduce some contrasting vivid colour, perhaps scarlet or emerald green, on the narrow inside edging (where the lid closes on to the chest). A small motif for the centre of the inside lid can be planned: this could engagingly include initials or a date, as seen on samplers. This would be particularly apt if your chest, as was traditional, is to celebrate a wedding or anniversary. Such pieces become family heirlooms with the passing of

Opposite: Part of a collection of co-ordinated furniture I designed, originally painted in a range of blues and greens and overlaid finally with black prior to stencilling. Below: The chest on which I first tried stencilling.

Opposite: *A Noah's Ark toy-box, using the same stencils as those designed for Jude's room (see p. 35), this time in yellow ochre on a dark-green ground, which gave it a strangely oriental look.* Opposite, above right: *A detail of the elephant from the side of the box.* Opposite, below right: *The head of the lion, with the palm stencilled over him.* Opposite, below left: *The dove from the top of the box, showing the effect of sanding down the top colour to allow the background to show through.*

A chest decorated with a sheaf of wheat. The broken braided panel emphasizes its elongated shape, and an additional border of wheat completes it, above and right.

The fox chair, showing in more detail how the stencil works with the grain of the chair's curved back.

time, valued because of the care and imagination devoted to them as much as for any exceptional skill or intrinsic value.

CHAIRS

A chair provides a simple base for some stencil-work and most people have a kitchen chair or wooden stool that would thrive with a little attention.

An idea for decorating the back of an old wooden armchair came to me from sighting a magnificent dog fox at close quarters one summer morning. The fox now blends into the treacly varnish of the chair which acts as a camouflage of bracken over-stencilled with grasses. Using the natural colouring of the fox I stretched my drawn fox full length in order to fit well into the shaped wooden back. I have six more plain country chairs to decorate with other field animals and some birds. A high chair could have a velvety mole, cut out amongst small earthy hillocks. The four-legged animals will fit, as the fox did, along the chair-backs, but the birds will need such devices as eggs and leaves to extend the length of the image.

Chair seats, with their diverse and subtle forms, are alternative areas for stencilling. Look carefully at their shape before deciding on decoration; round seats look well wreathed with leaves, while less regular shapes could carry some centrally placed design.

Doors and drawers are elements of the construction of so many pieces of furniture that it seems logical to set out the possibilities for stencilling these parts separately and leave it to you to select what is relevant to the piece you wish to work on.

It may help to regard a panelled door as a frame surrounding a flat central space which can be treated like a picture. Designs that are traditionally suited to doors include baskets of fruit, vases, posies, garlands of flowers (see p. 151), and birds on leafy branches.

When there is more than one panel concerned, the design can be repeated in each. It was in this way that I worked on an eight-panelled cupboard, using a peony stencil evolved from the design of the china that was kept inside it (a similar treatment appears on p. 150). The four top panels were slightly shorter than the bottom set, so the stencil needed a little judicious shortening. To complete the feeling of overall pattern that was on the china, I also stencilled the outside border with a simple design of fretwork.

When you are using the same stencil on a number of adjacent panels keep turning and reversing it in order to maximize any rhythmic variations in the design. However, if you are stencilling a large number of doors in the same room – as, for instance, on a kitchen unit – it is best to cut a number of different designs within the same theme so that the repetition does not become monotonous.

Don't forget knobs and handles. These can be removed before stencilling but, before removing them, assess whether you want to incorporate them into your design, since they can sometimes provide focal points.

It is a short step from mastering the challenge of a cupboard door to tackling one of a different scale, a door to a room. This may call for restraint, so consider confining yourself to one particular area of the house, such as the doors of a landing, and use patterns of a slightly classical nature. A wreathed border of oak leaves and acorns, for example, could be applied to their inner framework. Alternatively you could simply use a single design for each panel. Sometimes the main areas of design may be pulled together by adding a stencilled border or ribboned effect to the edge of each door, drawer or panel. This can be cut into the edge of the principal stencil, made up from a border and corner. Attention should be paid to the subtle contrivance of bridges on these borders to ensure that they have a free-flowing rhythm linking with the main motif.

One need not restrict oneself to this formal approach to the decoration of furniture. A less symmetrical, more organic look can also be achieved with stencils. One such example is a small chest of drawers for a bedroom which, when finished, appeared to have a pale lacy table-cloth lying over it. This 'cloth' had an overall design of wild flowers, clover, daisies, primroses and honeysuckle, edged with billows of cow parsley; it fell evenly patterned across the top of the whole structure, drawers, struts, top and sides. All handles had been removed before stencilling and the drawers wedged in place to ensure continuity in the design as it spread across the chest. Before the handles were replaced they too were decorated with heads of cow parsley.

When stencilling drawers, think out how you will manoeuvre the design around any protruding handles or locks. You may choose to set the design between the handles (or, alternatively, close to them), forming a focus like a ribboned rosette. If there is a pretty keyhole on a small drawer, a festoon of miniature flowers like scarlet pimpernels and forget-me-nots could be depicted swinging below it in a manner resembling Dresden china. It is usual with furniture for drawers to be in sets or pairs, so utilize to the full the strength that comes from repeating designs.

If you decorate drawers or doors in a complex manner, this may make the surrounding casing seem bare; it may then be worth considering putting some appropriate designs on the side.

With desks and bureaux one can also consider stencilling their interiors. A surprising element

could, perhaps, be introduced with an intricately worked Paisley pattern, which is apparent only when the flap is lowered.

TABLES

The variety and range of design possibilities for the many different types of table are enormous. Character and purpose should be carefully defined as an initial step towards resolving your design thinking. Stencilling will work well on pine or plainly painted tables. The most basic kitchen table on which the family take their daily meals can be effectively decorated. Rings of leaves and berries can, for example, be applied to mark out place-settings; calculate the number of places that will fit easily around your

Geraniums were used to decorate this table in a breakfast-room, above and below, *while a more overall effect is achieved,* opposite, *by using them on a variety of surfaces – walls, blind and the panels of the bed.*

table, spaced at a comfortable distance from each other, then spray the design on to each space. Napkins too could be stencilled with berries.

A round-topped dining-table could take a ring of larger scale, as on p. 142; this may be a garland of flowers placed inside the cutlery settings, leaving a space in the centre which, for special occasions, could also be filled with a bowl of cut fresh flowers.

Small occasional tables for sitting-rooms, and the taller variety for bedsides, are often the objects of restful contemplation and benefit from some treatment that is visually arresting. These could be enlivened with patterned borders or sprigged all over with small sprays of leaves and flowers in the manner of Victorian silks and muslins.

Black and other coloured lacquers were much favoured as a surface by Chinese stencillers, and they make a dramatic backcloth on which to work. I have stencilled a group of ivory-white lilies with their foil of curving coppery leaves on to a low black table, to good effect. A small vignette of a cage of canaries, hanging among pale willow leaves, could also look very good.

An interesting area to stencil on side tables (and, incidentally, sofas as well) is the apron which runs around beneath the top. I stencilled this area on a mahogany marble-topped wash stand with small clusters of bright Saxe-blue grapes against dark leaves, linked with braided turquoise ribbons. This now stands as a handsome side table.

BEDS

After a period when the divan bed was *de rigueur* and nothing much more than a shallow headboard was attached to its strict rectangle, a taste has emerged for something more elaborate; beds with high ends, half-testers, or full-blown four-posters. These, together with all their accompaniments, allow much more scope for stencil decoration. Such beds in fact can be simply constructed and made up around an existing divan, with stencilled headboards and hang-

ings added. We shall be looking at the various possibilities for stencilling the latter with coverlets, quilts and pillow-slips.

The flat areas of the end-panels of beds are good for stencilling, but long, winding designs can also be applied to rails and posts. Plants such as convolvulus, honeysuckle, hops and the vine can be attractively brought into play here.

I stencilled a French country bed of generous proportions with brilliant vermilion geraniums and dark-green leaves on the yellowing pine of its head and end (see p. 143). At the top I worked on the inside so that the flowers would appear around the pillows, while I decorated the outside panels of the foot so that the full length of the image could be clearly seen. The trunk could be decorated with the same stencils as the foot of the bed.

BEDS FOR BABIES AND CHILDREN

Children's beds may be stencilled to absorb the attention of restless infants; groups of familiar toys or animals could preoccupy early waking hours. It is easiest to dismantle the cot and work on it flat. The same stencils could be utilized to make a frieze around the walls at dado level, a good height for nursery friezes. Simple wooden cots on rockers may be figured with sleeping doves in pale tones, or with a brighter traditional Dutch-tulip design, such as that on page 151.

SHELVES

Shelves need little in the way of ornamentation; they are usually full of plates, books or other personal possessions as they perform their roles in dressers, bookcases, cabinets and corner cupboards. However, further embellishment can sometimes be appropriate and it would be easy to stencil a small motif dotted along the very edge of a shelf made to look like those mellow jagged cut-leather trims sometimes seen along old library shelving.

Louise and Harriet in their stencilled jackets.

always dye well, have a smooth surface and are available in different weights suitable for a variety of uses. I have also found some dull raw silks excellent (see p. 89), as they hold colour well.

For stencilling anything that requires day-to-day laundering, Dylon 'Colorfun' used in conjunction with a spray diffuser is the most suitable colouring agent. A spray diffuser is a small glass jar with two tubes protruding from its screw-topped lid; the larger of the tubes is blown through causing the paint to spray out of the finer one. Spray on to a piece of similar cloth with dye to check its direction and to see how hard you need to blow to cause a gentle variation of the colour on the fabric. The diffuser allows one to achieve a subtle blending of shades using different colours but it is important to wash out the diffuser well between each change of colour. You may prefer to begin your fabric printing by simply applying colour-dye through the stencil with a brush. If, however, you become very involved with spray-dying and stencils you may find it worth buying an air-brush which propels the dye with gas. Ironing over a clean cloth for one or two minutes with a hot iron will satisfactorily seal and fix the colour.

By comparison with screen-printing, where each colour requires a separate process of application, great variations of colour may be achieved in a short time. As an alternative to Dylon I find that spray paint, surprisingly, also works well on cloth, although I could not vouch for its survival in any long-term machine washing; dry-cleaning, or hand-washing would be safer.

On dressers, rosy plates could be propped against some leafy design on the boards behind them; the joins of the wooden boards break into the already fragmented stencil-work, which has the same appeal as the broken designs on a stencilled floor. Dressers with shaped apron fronts to their shelves could be stencilled with a design drawn from corn on the cob or some other shapely vegetable.

FABRICS

Stencilling fabric is no different in principle from any other form of stencilling. It provides a very simple way to create your own textiles. Natural fabrics work best: cotton, calico and linen are ideal since they

CUSHIONS

You may enjoy stencilling a single cushion to suit the colouring of a particular chair or sofa, or you may like to co-ordinate the decoration of a number of cushions of varied shapes and sizes. These could be stencilled with sprigs, circles and bunches of the same flowers, and have their edges piped in matching colours. Grouped at the head of a bed, or in a window seat,

A collection of country images used in diverse ways on fabric: the corner of a pillow case, above left; cushions and chair coverings, right; a circular tablecloth, below; and curtains and a bedcover, opposite.

these could form a most attractive addition to a stencilled room scheme.

Cane chairs can be made very pretty, and much more comfortable, with a cushioned inside shell; cut the shape from a sheet of one-inch foam to fit the curve around the back and sides; cover this with a fitted slip of calico, stencilled with a suitable motif. Sew on a few covered buttons at regular intervals to hold the foam in place; then stencil and make up a good plump cushion for a seat, finishing it with piping to match the buttons (dark green seems to suit this kind of furniture).

Another way to make a cushion from a stencil is to spray through the design on to tapestry canvas, then work the design in stitchery. A fine set of chair seats could be made in this manner, perhaps using a traditionally Dutch design of overblown tulips and rippling ribbons.

146

PILLOW-SLIPS

Pillow-slips look pretty with a little stencilling applied to them; corners could be printed with pale bunches of wild flowers or herbs. Buy the plain cases already made-up and slip a piece of card inside to lie under the part you are working on to prevent any unsightly bleeding-through of the dye on to the bottom layer. Stencil just one, or all, of the corners, and you may like to stitch some cotton lace around the edges, slotted with ribbon to match the flowers.

CURTAINS AND BLINDS

One of the most effective ways to use stencil-printed cloth is in conjunction with wall-stencilling; a frieze border could also form the edging on a pair of curtains and their ties. Equally a pattern could be devised and stencilled more generally, at a different scale.

There is something almost translucent about a stencilled fabric blind; the back-lighting throws up the image, with both softness and brightness operating together, and the fine firm canvas is extremely receptive to the sprayed-on shapes. A robust pot with a vigorous scarlet geranium takes up the full drop of the blind shown on p. 143.

Renewed enthusiasm for the four-poster bed gives scope for stencilled bed-hangings made up elaborately or plainly as curtains, complementing any accompanying quilt handsomely.

A four-poster in a country bedroom would look well with its curtains and canopy stencilled with a theme taken from Jacobean crewel-work. The rhythmical branches bearing a strange variety of leaves and fruit could be stencilled in strong colours on linen or heavy cotton. The fragmented nature of the stencilled image is not unlike the staccato stitchery of crewel-work, which would make this a particularly appropriate translation.

TABLECLOTHS

It is surprising how easy it is to make cheap and pretty tablecloths with stencils. They can be bought ready-made, or suitable cloth can be bought to make up. Long cloths that fall to the ground are especially pleasing to stencil.

If you are making your own cloth, it is a good idea to cut out a set of napkins at the same time, particularly if you are planning a circular cloth which leaves you with the waste of cut-away corners.

Rectangular cloths and napkins are easily stencilled with straight borders; however, some extra care should be taken to ensure that the design links together well when it meets at the corners. Check this out on a sheet of paper first; repeat a small in-filling design across the main ground of the cloth.

On circular cloths, edging borders need to be designed in a curve and the same design could also be used to form a ring around the top of the table. For large parties I cover long trestle tables with lengths of calico, stencilled down the sides with fruity garlands and ribbons; this festive look transforms them.

QUILTS

On the bed of the stencilled room at the American Museum near Bath there is a charming cotton coverlet stencilled in gentle colours; the pleasure derived from such an artefact would be well worth the time and care taken in producing it. If the idea of working directly on to such a large area strikes you as daunting, the whole thing could be divided into segments and stencilled in pieces; in this way it would not be too sad if certain parts had to be re-stencilled for better results. You may, for example, stencil the border in a strip and the centre portion in squares, then sew the whole thing together at the end, mounting it on a plain cotton base in the same way that many patchwork quilts were made up.

Indeed, you may feel so enthused by the results of your stencil-work that you go on to accentuate your design with quilting. You would, however, need to sandwich a layer of wadding between the two cloths in order to carry out such work. I have a quilt which has a stencilled and quilted central area and a deep plain border with carefully mitred corners.

FLOORS

Wooden floors make an ideal surface for stencilling, as the spray paint stains and bites into the unvarnished surface. It is preferable to strip any wooden floor back to the plain wood, which can be effectively tinted with a thinned water-based paint before stencilling.

To mark out a floor use the same principle as for walls. Borders are measured from the edge. For any in-fill designs find the centre by stretching strings diagonally from each corner. Plot relevant positions and mark them with pieces of masking-tape or chalk. Use a T-square to check right-angles.

After stencilling, seal over the floor with a minimum of three coats of matt or gloss clear polyurethane varnish, allowing twenty-four hours' drying time between each coat.

SCREENS

Screens are traditional objects for stencil decoration, and they are lovely to work on. A full-length design, cut as one stencil for the side of a panel, may be repeatedly used for all the panels. On the screen illustrated below, a whole design was carefully linked across to form a continuous picture.

Fire-screens, free-standing or fixed to seal off a disused fireplace, can really be improved with some stencilling. The free-standing variety could be stencilled with a cutaway shape; a basket of oranges glowing on black wood would cheer such a screen.

A screen can transform a room, disguising walls that cannot be altered.

An old French cupboard
in cherry wood, its panels
stencilled with a peony
design. Opposite: Vases
of tulips were stencilled
on the panels of this
green country cupboard.
The detail shows how
effectively colours can
be mixed.

MISCELLANEOUS

FRAMES

Frames for mirrors, photographs or pictures provide great scope for the stencilled border. I have stencilled a handsome heavy black oak frame to look like marquetry, with palm trees, little pavilions, strange mythical animals and hunting dogs; three stencils were necessary for the design to read vertically on every side.

If a frame is square and you visualize a plainly linking design, only the length of one side need be cut for a stencil (to be repeated four times). In such cases it is particularly advisable to make a trial print on paper to check that the corners form a clear and

well-designed change of direction. On an oblong frame an extra length will need to be added to the stencil for the two longer sides.

With a small frame (the width could be as little as one and a half inches) very delicate cutting is required and a bare minimum of a quarter of an inch is needed on each side of the design for attaching masking tape. Decorating the sides of a deep frame is also worth considering.

TRAYS, PICTURES AND GAMES BOARDS

Tin or wooden trays provide obvious grounds for all manner of stencil-work. A table used for board games might just as well have a stencilled chequered top, embellished with some formal border.

Velvet is the traditional background for a stencilled picture and the stencils used to decorate such pictures have their own particular name, 'theorems'. Stencil on to the velvet in the same way you would for any material; you may like to follow tradition by making a separate stencil for each colour. If you do, very careful placing of each stencil is necessary to ensure good registration.

STATIONERY, PAPERS AND FRIEZES

Paper is probably the easiest material to stencil since the faintest sprayed image shows up very distinctly and can have a highly appealing mottled quality. Cut your stencil, which may be quite small, from a sheet of card just larger than the paper you wish to decorate. This eliminates the need for elaborate masking. Stencil writing-paper and envelopes alike with very faint imagery. Stencil labels for files and cards for all occasions. The pineapple, as the symbol of hospitality, is particularly apt for invitation cards.

It is worth choosing a special-quality paper for hand-decorated stationery but, if you are stencilling a lining for a chest or cupboard, plain newsprint is more pliable and quite adequate for the job.

Consider stencilling room-friezes on strips of wall-

paper to be pasted round the top of a room after printing. This might work well for nervous stencillers, daunted by the prospect of working straight on to a wall; any faulty stencilling can be cut away and discarded, and a new length printed off. Small sprigged patterns, sparsely placed, are most effective for wallpaper, particularly when used in conjunction with a friezed border.

Stencil wrapping-papers for Christmas. Buy sheets of plain shop wrapping-paper to work on, as this will be the right weight and texture; cut a stencil design of the same size. Plain boxes and paper 'ribbons' could be stencilled to match each other; metallic paints can be fun to use.

LAMPSHADES

Lampshades, when illuminated, show up the delicately speckled colour variation of sprayed stencil-work. Cut a template by wrapping a sheet of cartridge paper around your existing frame and cut accurately along its edges and seams. Use these shapes to design and cut your stencils. When applying, spray the prepared stencil with adhesive and attach it to the frame with masking tape, then lightly spray with colour. Alternatively, if you are making your own shade, stencil the shaped sections of your material while flat, attaching it to the frame afterwards.

CANVAS CHAIRS AND TENTS

Old faded canvas can be removed from deck-chairs and a new length measured out from it. Stencil this with bees around a hive or a large pot of pelargoniums and fix it back into position with new brass upholstery tacks. Waterproof canvas garden or boat cushions are fun to stencil. Stencil both sides as they are likely to be turned over.

Think of your tent as a painter's canvas. A child's tent could be stencilled around with clowns and circus animals, or a wild 'Red Indian' theme of buffalo, eagles, bows and arrows.

BAGGAGE

Individually stencilled canvas luggage is easily identified on luggage racks and in customs sheds. Satchels and hold-alls, trunks or rucksacks bearing markings or initials are instantly recognized as one's own. To transform a plain piece of luggage, why not simulate the richness of a carpet-bag with a pattern taken from a Turkish rug?

The areas to be decorated can be smoothed out and the stencil attached with spray glue as usual. Protect and waterproof them. Leather can be stencilled with shoe dye, applied through a diffuser.

METAL

Kitchen equipment such as fridges can be cold, unappealing objects to look at, but consider the plain surfaces imprinted with some basket-work design and the freezer-top spilling over with vegetables. Spray paint sold primarily for applying to car bodies is ideal for metal surfaces. Filing cabinets can be made to merge better with a room's décor. It is obvious that one need not restrict decoration to a kitchen canister or a filing cabinet; having first practised on such items, you will see that the results can be immaculate enough for you to attempt an exclusive emblem for your car door or even a discreet leafy camouflage for your caravan.

Above and opposite, above: Some of my painted furniture with linking country imagery.

Below: A black mirror frame decorated with gilded birds, leaves and berries.

STENCILLING MATERIALS

DRAWING AND DESIGN

Sketch-pad or cartridge paper, pencil and rubber. Felt-tip pens or watercolours – for designing and colouring.

DRAWING UP THE STENCIL

Stencil-card – canary-yellow (or sometimes tan) manila card which has been previously saturated in linseed oil, then dried. A smooth surface, very easy to cut.

Fine felt-tip pen – for marking out on the stencil-card areas of design which are to be cut away.

CUTTING THE STENCIL

Red Stanley craft-knives (these are lightweight, and with their mildly flexible plastic handles, can be manoeuvred easily). They are cheap and disposable, so no need to work with a blunt blade.

Work-boards – purpose-made, self-healing cutting mats are ideal; alternatively linoleum or vinyl tiles can be used.

ATTACHING THE STENCIL

Ruler or tape-measure – for accurate positioning.

Masking tape – for positioning the stencil, and attaching newsprint masking.

White chalk – useful for marking the position of a design on to furniture, floors and other surfaces.

Aerosol adhesive – for attaching the stencil closely to the surface. Blu-Tack – for attaching the stencil to hard (metal) surfaces.

Fine pins and tack-hammer – for pinning the stencil flat on to any receptive surface instead of using spray glue.

Lining-paper – to form an extended mask around the stencil as a protection against the drift of paint spray. It is useful also for testing sprays and as a protective surface when spraying the stencil with spray glue.

SPRAYING

'DupliColor' or 'Car Plan' spray paint – suitable for application to almost any surface. Extensive colour range that includes metallic paint. Tough and fast drying.

Dylon 'Colour-fun' – a dye suitable for stencilling on cloth. Diffuser – for applying dye.

Disposable paper mask – should be used when applying spray paint in an enclosed space.

Tissues – for wiping the nozzles of paint canisters clean after use (to ensure that they do not spatter or clog when next used).

Nail varnish remover – helps to clear the nozzles if paint has dried; a good solvent for cleaning any paint from hands, or for washing a brush after detailing.

DETAILING AND FINISHING

Fine sable brush – occasionally needed for minute detailing.

Furniture polish – for integrating stencil-work on a wooden surface.

Polyurethene wood seal – for protecting stencilled floors. Available in gloss, satin or matt finishes.

Decorators' glaze – protection for emulsioned walls, useful for eliminating the shine of the stencilled image on such a surface.

SUPPLIERS

Manila card, cutting-mats, craft knives; catalogue of
stencil designs; prospectus for stencilling courses.
Lyn Le Grice Stencil Design Ltd, Bread St. Penzance,
Cornwall TR18 2EQ (Tel: 0736 69881). Mail order
service.

'DupliColor' spray paint.
At Pep Boys Stores and other automotive supplies stores
nationwide.

Varnishes, specialist paints, brushes, etc.
Janovich Plaza, 1150 Third Avenue, New York, New
York 10021 (Tel: 212-517-7000). Mail order service.
Pearl Paint Co., Inc., 308 Canal Street, New York, New
York 10007 (Tel: 212-431-7932)

Scotch 'SprayMount'.
Charette Drafting Supplies, 215 Lexington Avenue, New
York, New York 10016 (Tel: 212-683-8822)
Sam Flax, 111 Eighth Avenue, New York, New York
10011 (Tel: 212-620-3000). Mail order service.

Many of the materials mentioned in the text will be
found at local artist's suppliers, stationery, hobby and
hardware stores.

SUGGESTED FURTHER READING

Adèle Bishop and Cile Lord, *The Art of Decorative Stencilling*, Thames & Hudson, London, 1976.

Clarence P. Hornung, *Treasury of American Antiques*, Harry N. Abrams, New York, 1977

Jocasta Innes, *The Pauper's Homemaking Book*, Penguin Books, Harmondsworth, 1976.

Jocasta Innes, *Paint Magic*, Winward, Leicester, 1983

Russell H. Kettell, *Early American Rooms 1650–1858*, Dover Publications, New York, 1968

Jean Lipman, *Techniques in American Folk Decoration*, Dover Publications, New York, 1972

Jean Lipman and Alice Winchester, *The Flowering of American Folk Art 1776–1876*, Viking Press, New York; Thames & Hudson, London, 1974

Andrew W. Tuer, *Japanese Stencil Designs*, Dover Publications, New York, 1968

Janet Waring, *Early American Stencils on Walls and Furniture*, Dover Publications, New York, 1968.

The following selection of books and articles offers useful general, mostly visual, information for devising stencils based on traditional designs and natural subjects:

Arts Council, *Islamic Carpets from the Joseph V. McMullan Collection: Catalogue*, London, 1972

James Ayres, *British Folk Art*, Barrie & Jenkins, London, 1977

David Black, *Islemeler: Ottoman Domestic Embroideries*, D. Black Oriental Carpets, London, 1978

Peter Coats, *Great Gardens of the Western World*, Putnam, New York, 1963

Joan Edwards, *Crewel Embroidery in England*, Batsford, London, 1975

E. A. Entwistle, *Literary History of Wallpaper*, Batsford, London, 1960

Ralph Fastnedge, *English Furniture Styles*, Penguin Books, Harmondsworth, 1968

Sir Harry Garner, *Chinese Lacquer*, Faber & Faber, London, 1979

Mark Girouard, *Historic Houses of Britain*, Morrow, New York, 1979

Desmond Guinness and William Ryan, *Irish Houses and Castles*, Thames & Hudson, London, 1979

Victor and Takake Hauge, *Folk Traditions in Japanese Art*, Kodansha International, Kyoto, 1978, in co-operation with the International Exhibitions Foundation, Washington, D.C., and the Japanese Foundation Victor and Audrey Kennett, *The Palaces of Leningrad*, Thames & Hudson, London, 1973

Andreas Lommel, *Prehistoric and Primitive Man*, Hamlyn, London, 1966

Eva Mannering (ed.), *Redoute Fruits and Flowers*, Ariel Press, London, 1977

Eadweard Muybridge, *Animals in Motion*, Dover Publications, New York, 1957

David Nickerson, *English Eighteenth Century Furniture*, Weidenfeld & Nicolson, London, 1963

Nigel Nicolson, *Great Houses of the Western World*, Putnam, New York, 1968

Seiroku Noma, *Japanese Costume and Textile Arts*, Weatherhill, Salem, Massachusetts, 1975

Francis W. Reader, 'Use of the Stencil in Mural Decoration', *Journal of the Archaeological Society*, Vol. 95, No. 1, 1938

Carleton L. Safford and Robert Bishop, *America's Quilts and Coverlets*, Dutton, New York, 1980

SOME STENCILS TO CUT OUT

Here and on the following pages are my 'Thrift' and border stencils for you to use. Trace the designs and transfer them to stencil card. Then cut out the shapes and spray-paint through them, as described on pp. 124–33.

ACKNOWLEDGEMENTS

PHOTOGRAPHIC ACKNOWLEDGEMENTS

All the photographs in this book are by David Cripps except:

Page 8, Victoria and Albert Museum, London; page 9, left, Musée de l'Homme, Paris; page 10, James Austin (courtesy of Colchester Borough Council); page 11, top and bottom left, S. G. Sefton; page 11, bottom right, James Austin; page 14, left, reproduced by permission of James Ayres, Freshford, Bath; page 16, top, R.I.B.A. Drawings Collection; page 17, left, University of Glasgow; page 17, right, Annan.